PICTURE GALLERY PIONEERS

PICTURE GALLERY PIONEERS

1850 to 1875

By Ralph W. Andrews

(Opposite) **EADWEARD J. MUY-BRIDGE** resting against a Mariposa redwood after his labors in Yosemite, in 1872.

BONANZA BOOKS · NEW YORK

Power ceases in the instant of repose;
it resides in the moment of
transition from a past to a
new state, in the shooting of the
gulf, in the darting to a new aim. . . .

EMERSON

Foreword

When I started work on this book and mentioned to several persons that the project concerned early photographers, their response was usually along this line— "That should be interesting. They didn't have much to work with, did they?"—or "Early photographers? Are enough people interested in early methods like that?"

What this meant to me was, those people seemed to be more interested in photography than photographers. To make a general observation, I think book readers today pay more attention to the mechanics of a subject than to the people behind the mechanics. It is not uncommon for a reader to finish a book full of technical details yet not know the names of persons mentioned in the book or even who wrote it. Yet one of the precepts of all writing is—people are interested in people. Is there a trend away from this in our mechanical age?

At any rate this is a photo-history about photo people, the first in their field, stalwarts in a new trade who had enterprise and courage, two qualities I admire above all others in men. To think of these young fellows emigrating to the new West with little assurance of being able to make a living with their crude cameras . . . to think of them working against all kinds of difficulties, including public skepticism—suggested all the elements of romance and that meant I had to do something about it.

I found also, when I told friends about this book, that they had the same idea of "early" photographers as I did ten years ago. My first photo-history, *This Was Logging*, concerned the work of Darius Kinsey, the great photographer of Washington timber and the logging industry. At that time I considered him "early," and so he was, about 1885 to 1920. What then was T. H. O'Sullivan, who helped make Matthew Brady famous, and C. E. Watkins who took pictures in the California placer mines fifteen years before the Civil War? Early? A relative term certainly.

I did not expect these pioneer technicians to produce photographs of quality and when I found several of them did, achieved under every adverse circumstance, I felt nothing but sheer admiration for their artistry and industry. Some of those pioneers were turning out photographs 100 years ago that put some modern stuff to shame.

I take little credit for finding the material you see and read in the book. About all I did was point and librarians, historical society staffs and individual collectors did the finding. Of inestimable help were Grace Dobbins of the Salt Lake Public Library, Dale Walden in Boise and Robert Weinstein of Los Angeles. Opal Harber, James Davis and the staff of the Denver Public Library, Western History Department, were very helpful as was John Barr Tompkins and his people at Bancroft Library, University of California.

Let me publicly thank also, for their substantial aid, Robert Monroe, Head of Special Collections at the University of Washington Library; Margaret Shepherd of the Utah Historical Society; Dr. Merle Wells and staff of the Idaho Historical Society; Harriett Meloy of the Montana Historical Society; Dr. Ruth Mahood of the Los Angeles County Museum; Jerry MacMullen, Director Junipero Serra Museum in San Diego; the staffs of California State Library, Yosemite Park Museum, Society of California Pioneers, California Historical Society and Oregon Historical Society.

RALPH W. ANDREWS

CONTENTS

The Survey Photographers

1867-1873

LOOKING ACROSS COLORADO RIVER TO MOUTH OF PARIA CREEK. O'Sullivan photo on Wheeler Expedition.

T. H. O'SULLIVAN

In the early morning mists of July 4, 1863, a Union Army photographer set up his cumbersome instrument on a bloody battlefield and made one of the famous pictures of history—"The Harvest of Death." It depicted bodies of the Confederates strewn across the grass and was made by one of the men who helped perpetuate the fame of Matthew Brady as "the Civil War photographer"—T. H. O'Sullivan.

Little is known of the man prior to the war but his work after it includes some of the finest Western scenes of the early days. The war experience toughened him and tested his courage. Twice his camera was struck by shell fragments and again his camera cloth torn by shot and sand blown across his plates. His skill at taking pictures under fire brought him to the attention of government authorities organizing post-war surveys of the New West.

The early explorations beyond the Mississippi River were essentially geographic, concerned with locating and mapping lands and rivers. After the Civil War the objectives were broadened to gather geologic and ethnographic data. Among specific aims was scientific knowledge of Indian life. The government was attempting to destroy the Western tribes but there was sufficient official interest to realize the value of accurate records of Indian customs and behavior during their latter days.

The first important survey for these purposes was the United States Geological Expedition of the Fortieth Parallel under the direction of Clarence King and it included the experienced O'Sullivan as photographer. The survey started in Western Nevada, July 1, 1867 and continued for several years, O'Sullivan being with it through 1869.

The first party of explorers visited the Nevada mining camps, taking pictures of Nevada City and of the Comstock Lode activity when at its height. O'Sullivan went into the mines and made pictures in the black depths, using burning magnesium wire for light, probably the first interior mine views ever made. As the expedition moved eastward along the 40th Parallel through the Nevada wastelands, photographs were made of the Humboldt and Carson Sinks, the Ruby Range, and further east, of the twisting Snake River. Of these experiences, O'Sullivan wrote:

"It was a pretty location to work in, and *viewing* there was as pleasant work as could be desired; the only drawback was an unlimited number of the most voracious and particularly poisonous mosquitos that we met with during our entire trip. Add to this the entire impossibility to save one's precious body from frequent attacks of that most enervating of all fevers, known as the 'mountain ail', and you will see why we did not work up more of that country. We were, in fact, driven out by the mosquitos and fever. Which of the two should be considered as the most unbearable it is impossible to state."

What O'Sullivan did not speak of here was the laborious work of taking the pictures. He must carry with him into narrow defiles, down rivers and canyon bottoms, not only his camera but his dark room and all his supplies—glass, collodion, silver nitrate, developer. The plate must be flowed with collodion, sensitized in a dark tent or improvised chamber, exposed ten to thirty seconds and hurried back to the dark room for developing and a new plate prepared.

In 1870, T. H. O'Sullivan photographed the Isthmus of Panama on Commander Selfridge's survey for the proposed ship canal, known as the Darien Expedition, but the next year he was back in the United States with Lieut. George M. Wheeler's surveyors in the Southwest, and again in 1873 and 1874. During this last year he made photographs of particular elegance depicting the pueblo ruins in New Mexico's Canon de Chelle, which were used as the basis of many lithograph illustrations.

Later O'Sullivan succeeded E. Walker as chief photographer of the Treasury Department in Washington and succumbed to tuberculosis, January 14, 1882 at the home of a relative in Staten Island, N.Y.

VIRGINIA CITY, NEVADA in its former glory—O'Sullivan photo.

**MEMBERS ENGINEERING DEPART-
MENT** U.S. Geological Expedition of the 40th Parallel. O'Sullivan photo.

15

(*Upper*) **LAKE IN UINTA MOUN-TAINS, IDAHO.**

SHOSHONE FALLS in Snake River.
Both O'Sullivan photos.

GOLD HILL, NEVADA. (Note
O'Sullivan's dark room in lower left).

(*Upper*) **DONNER SUMMIT, CAL-
IFORNIA.** Both O'Sullivan photos.

17

CANON DE CHELLE, Arizona,
looking east. Hillers photo.

JOHN K. HILLERS

Only two of the three boats lasted out the arduous trip, one or more were capsized several times and one at least was sucked into a whirlpool. Despite dangers and hazards, the expedition brought back the first photographs ever taken inside the walls of the Grand Canyon of the Colorado River.

In 1869, John W. Powell, with a small party, had descended the previously unknown Colorado through its majestic canyon. Impressed by this notable feat, the government employed him for a number of years to explore the region in further detail.

The second Powell Expedition was fitted out in 1871, with photographer E. A. Beaman and Clement Powell as assistant. Jack Hillers was hired as boatman and handyman. He had served with the artillery in the Civil War, worked with the Brooklyn police force until his brother became sick and had to be removed to California. He took a job driving an overland freight outfit but yielded to the lure of gold, and with his ailing brother started for the mining camps.

Stopping in a Santa Fe hotel one night, they overheard through the thin partition, a conversation in an adjoining room—that of Major Powell and members of his party talking of their coming expedition. Jack Hillers knocked at the door of their room, told of his need for work to support his sick brother and so impressed Major Powell with his sturdiness and drive he was hired immediately.

The party left Green River, Wyoming, on May 22, 1871, and photographer Beaman remained with it for the first half of the trip, leaving when the boats—the *Emma Dean, Nellie Powell* and *Canonita*—were ready to start down the Colorado proper. Clement Powell tried to carry the photography burden but Hillers, who had shown an interest in the work and had been allowed to take some pictures, developed a skill so rapidly he had better results than Powell.

With the loss of Beaman, leader John W. Powell sent the younger Powell to Salt Lake City for James Fennemore, a capable and well known photographer. He joined the party, made a point of training the eager Jack Hillers who shortly was assisting him in all the photography. In the spring of 1872, Fennemore was taken sick, went home and Hillers was made photographer-in-chief.

Despite the difficulties under which Hillers worked, the photographs taken by him are regarded by authorities as equal to those taken later with better equipment and under more favorable circumstances and are highly valued as historical documents. Neither the dry plate nor easily carried film roll had been invented. Photographs were taken by the wet plate process. The photographer carried as many glass plates, covered with an albuminous substance, as he had pictures to take. When he was ready to make an exposure he would coat one of the plates with collodion, which formed a film to hold the silver solution with which it was covered. The plate had to be exposed while it was wet and developed within a few hours. After it was dry, it was varnished as a protection against injury and carefully packed in a grooved box to await the day when prints could be made.

The photographic apparatus J. K. Hillers used consisted of six hundred glass plates, some of them nearly a quarter of an inch think; several cameras, one of them designed to take the popular stereoscopic pictures; quantities of collodion, silver solution, developing and fixing chemicals, and varnish. Added to these was a "crazy old dark room," as Hillers described it, which he made of canvas and wood after Beaman left the expedition with his own dark room. This equipment, packed in rubber sacks and canvas-covered wooden boxes, was divided and stored in waterproof compartments in the three boats.

"During the day," Hillers is quoted as saying, "I

(Above left) **POWELL SURVEY CAMP AT GREEN RIVER CITY, WYOMING,** and right—**UTE WOMAN WITH JOHN W. POWELL.** All Hillers photos.

(Opposite) **GATE OF LODORE,** Green River, Wyoming.

would take my pictures, and when night came and the boats were tied at the river bank, I would get out my dark room and chemicals and develop the plates. Sometimes there would be enough light from a wood fire reflected down to the water to permit me to work. When there was no place to build a fire, someone would hold a lantern back of the light opening, and I would poke my head under the canvas and get to work. I missed a lot of sleep this way. When the water in the Colorado was muddy, we would watch for a clear stream emptying into the river and get a few bottles of fresh water for some of the finer work."

21

PUEBLO RUINS IN CANON DE CHELLE, ARIZONA. (Note figure of man in lower ruins.) Hillers photo.

YOSEMITE VALLEY, CALIFORNIA. Hillers photo.

WILLIAM H. JACKSON

"There is a mountain in the distant West
That, sun-defying, in its deep ravines
Displays a cross of snow upon its side."

The words are Longfellow's and the subject was Mount of the Holy Cross in Colorado's Rocky Mountains. And, as legend has it, his inspiration came from a photograph of the mountain made by William H. Jackson in 1873 which was contained in the report of the Hayden Survey of that year. It was one of the photographer's most famous pieces of work.

He had many famous ones—and most of these were the first made in those areas. Jackson has been called the "Father of Yellowstone National Park" and justifiable or not, it does appear fact that the photographs he made there were placed on exhibition in the halls of Congress and had a definite influence on the passage of the bill in 1872, which when signed by President Grant, created Yellowstone National Park.

Jackson's pictures of the West are known above all others. He had an artistic sense as a fine arts painter and sketcher, an appreciation for all the wonders of the outdoors and when he caught their images in his camera he was already an accomplished craftsman. It was his fortune that the country in which Dr. F. V. Hayden was making geological surveys was also "Jackson's country" and that he was engaged as official photographer for the survey work.

William Jackson was a youth in Vermont when rebellion broke out in the South and he enlisted in the Union Army from there. His home was in Troy, N.Y., his birthplace McKeeseville of that state. Photography was a natural interest to him since his father experimented with the daguerreotype process and at an early age, the boy showed an aptitude for drawing and painting when taught by his mother, a talented artist.

A broken love affair sent the ex-soldier West after the war, in 1866, and he kept diaries of his travels to Salt Lake City and California. The following year he brought a herd of broncos to the frontier town of Omaha on the Missouri River. His brother Edward, a professional photographer, joined him there in the firm of Jackson Brothers which prospered to the extent of absorbing the gallery of a competitor.

In 1866 the call of the outdoors was too strong to resist and William fitted up a dark room on a buckboard and went photographing Pawnee and Omaha Indians in Western Nebraska and Kansas. The next year he prospected views along the just completed line of the Union Pacific Railroad and sold the company many pictures along the route from Omaha to Salt Lake.

It was on the Hayden Survey of 1870 that Jackson Canyon, southwest of the present Casper, Wyoming, was named after the photographer. The expedition that year followed chiefly the Oregon Trail through Wyoming, passing Independence Rock, Fort Bridger and South Pass. Encamped in the latter region were the Shoshones of Chief Washakie and Jackson did extensive work in the tepee villages. Later he was to broaden the scope of his Indian pictures and publish a comprehensive catalog of his and other Indian views and portraits.

The Survey of 1871 took the party through the wonders of the Yellowstone which had been "discovered" by two earlier expeditions. Hayden covered nearly all the scenic marvels, beginning with Mammoth Hot Springs, Old Faithful, the Grand Canyon of the Yellowstone, and Jackson recorded them on plate. After the Hayden work ended, he continued his own travel and photographic work from a studio in Denver. He visited the Ute Indian Reservation and made pictures of Chief Ouray, Chipeta and other tribesmen.

OPHIR CITY, COLORADO. Both Jackson photos.

(*Opposite*) **WILLIAM H. JACKSON** on Glacier Point, Yosemite.

27

(*Opposite top*) **ANCIENT RUINS** in Canyon of the Mancos, Mesa Verde National Park. Bottom, **HAYDEN SURVEY CAMP** on Medicine Bow River.

W. H. JACKSON on Hayden Survey.

LOOKING NORTH ON BERTHOUD PASS, Colorado. All Jackson photos.

RUINS in the Canyon of the Mancos, Mesa Verde National Park.

(*Opposite*) PROVO FALLS, UTAH. (Note man's figure on ledge in center.)

COLORADO ELK, CERVUS CAN-ADENSIS. All Jackson photos.

WHITE MOUNTAIN HOT SPRINGS—group of upper basin, Yellowstone National Park.

(Above) **CASTLE GEYSER AND HOT SPRINGS**—Five Hole Basin, Yellowstone.

HAYDEN SURVEY CAMP on divide between Yellowstone Lake and East Fork. All Jackson photos.

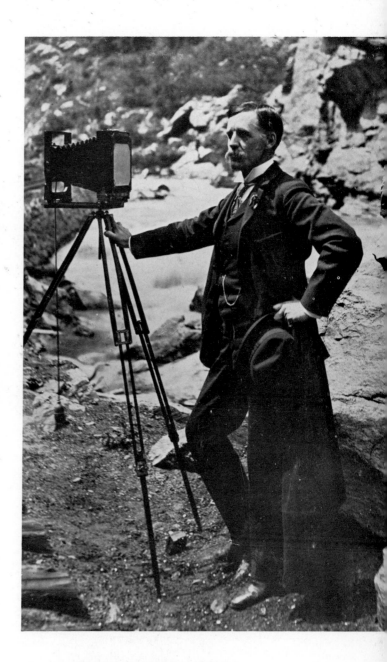

(*Opposite top*) **INTERIOR OF JACKSON'S** Denver studio on West Colfax Avenue.

(*Opposite bottom*) **THE OLD CARRETA,** Laguna, New Mexico.

WILLIAM H. JACKSON in 1890 at Camera Club outing. All Jackson photos.

VALLEY OF THE YELLOWSTONE. Jackson photo.

Portrait in a Gallery

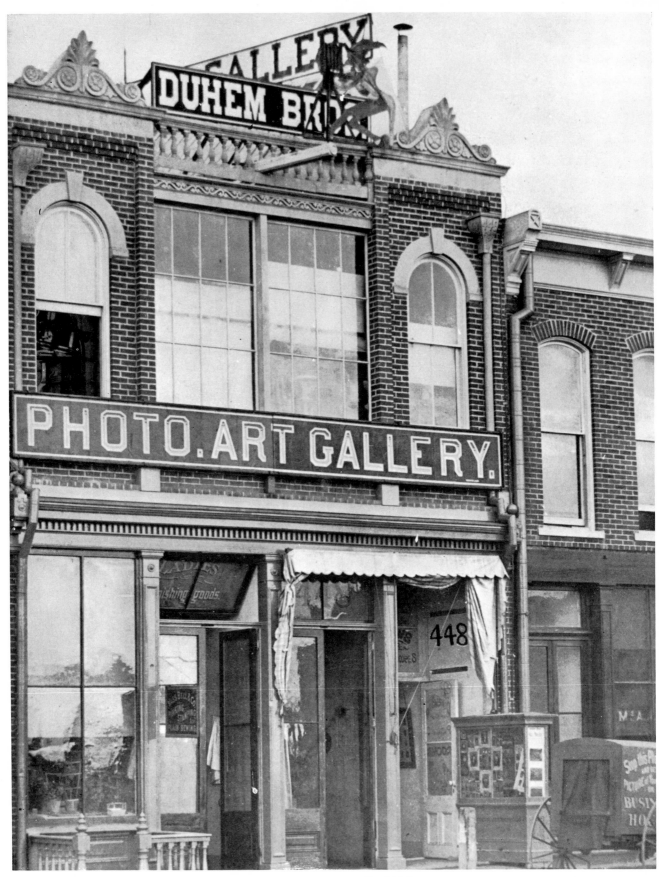

DUHEM BROTHERS GALLERY, DENVER.

Portrait in a Gallery

The advertising was lavish, the appeals bubbling out of a well-spring of extravagant rhetoric. And it was effective because sun-light pictures were as new and exciting as the rococo words that described them. Then too, you thought Ira Hotchkiss not too vain a man and he had taken his family to Mancroft's Gallery for a group portrait. It would be entirely tasteful if you did too. What was that advertisement again?

PICTURES BY THE
SUN'S PURE RAYS

Mancroft & Co.
Over Bittleman's Store on
Front Street

Using only the clear sun and clean air of our new mountain city to furnish you the most exquisite Photographs, Ambrotypes, Enameled Cards, Sun Pearls, Cartes de Visite to swell your heart with joy. Each picture is a gem of highest magnitude. Our artists are skilled with brush and pen. Our rooms are marvels of luxury and elegance. Our only thought is to palpitate your pride. Our pledge is to satisfy all who favor us with a call.

VIEWS OF BUILDINGS & SCENERY TAKEN

Yes, you knew such notable persons as H. M. Don Pietro, Emperor of Brazil, Sir Oliver Bundy, Susan B. Arthur and Ralph Waldo Emeritus had sat for Mancroft and the man had done a cracking good job. It should be no difficulty getting Anabelle to the studio although convincing her that this photography was no novelty that would wear off in a few months was another thing. Yet she must realize that people of quality were accepting it as stylish and she would look very pretty in her new taffeta dress with the modish train. How nice it would be to have a suitable picture of Anabelle and you and the baby to send back to the family in Philadelphia.

In the end it worked out very smoothly. You were in Bittleman's store to get new shoes and so walked up the long flight of stairs to Mancroft's Gallery above it, and made the appointment with the clerk. Wednesday at three would be very good and Mr. Mancroft himself would handle the camera instead of one of the assistants.

"You are Mr. Chambers, the banker, are you not, sir?" the clerk asked with oily concern. "May I make a suggestion? Mr. Mancroft would want you to know the best mode of dress for a portrait. Yes, sir. Dark brown, dark green, maroon and plain black goods, without gloss—for ladies, of course, sir—give the richest effect. Silks of those colors will take considerably lighter. Now, snuff brown, dark leather, dark drab, or scarlet, cherry, dark orange, crimson and slate will also take well. But violet, blue, purple, pink and magenta will take very light and should be avoided. The hair, to take well, should never be wet or glossy. I am sure Mrs. Chambers will appreciate knowing this. Yes, thank you, sir."

On Wednesday you had the carriage come for the three of you and Anabelle did look darling. Even her sister in Harrisburg would be charitable when she saw this picture. At least you told Anabelle so because she was still expecting some sort of ordeal like having a bunion cut off. The baby was fidgety but you thought Mancroft's "marvels of luxury" would include a rattle or toy to keep him occupied. And Anabelle complained about climbing the long flight of stairs, turning to you halfway up. "Henry—what is that unconscionable odor?" You were quite aware of it yourself and put it down as the acids and solutions used in the business, perhaps with some skunk oil added for emphasis.

An iron horse weight held the studio door open and the fumes were intensified so much that your eyes almost burned. Yet Anabelle was not complaining now, her eyes wide open with wonder just as you hoped they would be. Mancroft's reception room was big, at least fifty feet square and elaborately furnished with sofas, chairs, easels and tables, the walls hung with some of his spectacular mountain views in heavy gilt frames. A basket of stereopticon cards was placed on a small taboret with the sighting instrument beside it. And then Mr. Mancroft was bounding up and rubbing his hands together like the Greek wine seller you saw in London, his little bald head bobbing obsequiously.

"I am so happy to have you come to me, Mr. Chambers and lady. And this is the little man. The small Chambers, as it were—hah, hah. I must have my little joke. Now I am ready for you. Will you step this way please."

You followed him through the doorway into a smaller room lit brightly by a huge sky-light which covered half the ceiling and half of one wall. Arranged around the other wall space were great easels on casters bearing garish representations of castles and forests and river scenes painted on canvas. And in the center of the room, was the huge camera, dominating everything but the monkey-like boundings of Mr. Mancroft.

"Now, Mr. Chambers, will you stand by this settee—here in front of the Grecian column on the backdrop. Your lady will sit here. The sun is bright today and the picture will be very good. The baby —let me see—on a rug. The very thing. He will not be afraid of a bear? Emil—bring the white bear rug. There—spread it there. Ah, you see he is fascinated at once. What is the little fellow's name? Terence. See, Terence, the big head. Ah, no—he will not bite. Feel the nice thick fur. Yes, milady Chambers, you will sit here, please?"

Now Anabelle was ruffled again as obviously she did not like Mr. Mancroft's fluttery ways, and you were not particularly taken with them yourself. He had no sooner adjusted her head in the position he wanted than she broke her posture to lean over and speak to Terence. But after bouncing out from under the black camera cloth a number of times, lifting Terence and plumping him down against his mother's knee where she could hold his shoulders, he gave a final look at his three captives and dashed to the camera once more.

"Now, now—" the bald head disappeared again under the cloth and then popped out—"oh, smile, smile. You see my finger? Do not look at anything else. Do not look at Emil when he brings in the plate. Terence—see the finger wiggle, wiggle-wiggly—there, there—"

Without pausing in his sing-song talk he called Emil again. "Everybody is happy? Oh, yes—smile, milady Chambers. See the finger wiggle, Terence. Smile, Mr. Chambers. Now, Emil," He slipped a brass cap over the camera lens as Emil appeared with a flat case which he inserted into the back of the camera. Then Mr. Mancroft made final scrutiny of the group, frowning slightly at Anabelle's wrinkling nose, made a theatrical flourish as he removed the brass cap and pulled a black slide from the rear of the camera. He continued to make half-circles to punctuate his cheery talk and wiggles of the finger, counting with his taps of his left foot until he capped the lens and pushed the slide into the plate case.

"Now," announced the master with a short bow, "while Emil prepares another plate we will get ready for a position a little different. And milady Chambers, I must have a picture of you alone."

*   *   *

Patrons of the old-time photograph gallery rarely saw the mysteries behind the operating rooms. The photographer's assistant worked in a small dark room lighted only by a yellow gas flame. A coat-ing of silver nitrate covered walls and equipment. The assistant wore black overalls and worked with rubber gloves.

To prepare a plate for the photographic impression, he wiped a square of crown glass free of dust and holding it by the upper left hand corner, poured a thinly viscous fluid over it, inclining the plate gently from side to side to cover it evenly without streaks, letting the excess fluid drain back into the bottle. In less than a minute the fluid had dried to a varnish-like film. The fluid, iodized collodion, had been made by dissolving gun-cotton in ether and alcohol, with some iodide of ammonium added. The film represented organic matter from the cotton with the iodide of ammonium, after the volatile ether and alcohol had evaporated.

The plate was then lowered gently into a nitrate of silver bath where it must remain for three or four minutes. A decomposition took place there which changed the iodide of ammonium to iodide of silver, filling the pores of the collodion film and making it sensitive to light. The use of the collodion was to supply a delicate, homogenous, adhesive and colorless layer in which the iodide might be deposited, the film becoming in appearance like boiled white of egg. The plate was placed in a case protected from light by a shield so that it could be carried into the operating room and put in the camera in place of the ground glass through which the camera operator sighted his inverted image. When the slide or shield was removed and the brass cap taken off the lens, the plate was exposed.

When the assistant returned the plate to the dark room he poured a solution of proto-sulphate of iron on the white surface of the film, now carrying an image. After a time a change took place, light appearing in the picture where shadow had been, and vice versa. The plate was then held under running water and if the picture needed more contrast or definition, this was secured by intensifying or redeveloping. A solution of equal quantities of silver nitrate and pyrogallic acid was poured on the pictured film, the excess run back into the vessel, the process perhaps repeated several times. When again well washed with running water, the plate was immersed in a hyposulphate of soda bath which removed all the iodide of silver and left only the image of the film. After a few minutes the plate was again washed under the running stream of water, then dried and varnished. The finished result was a negative.

In these early days a special printing paper was imported from Europe. The photographer coated it with albumen, made from egg whites in a special process, and allowed it to dry. Each day some

KINGSLEY photograph of his young wife taken in his Idaho City studio.

of this albumenized paper was prepared for that day's prints. It was gently and deftly laid on the surface of a silver nitrate solution for a few minutes, drained and hung by one corner to dry. It was necessary to prepare the paper fresh each morning as it quickly lost its delicacy.

To make the print, a piece of the prepared paper was laid on the varnished side of the negative which was held in a wooden frame. A thick piece of cloth was laid on the paper and this covered by a hinged wooden form which pressed all parts together by means of two brass springs. The frame, or probably several, were set out in the sun, the operator checking each one after a time to see how the images were appearing. When one reached the proper shades of contrast, it was turned over with its back to the light.

These pictures, printed in the sunshine, were of a peculiar purple tint and it was necessary to put them through a series of processes in the dark to fix and tone them. After drying they were pasted to a card of the required size. The process for enlarging involved throwing the enlarged image from a negative down through a lens above a sheet of sensitive paper placed on a table which could be elevated or lowered. The image, weakened by diffusion over so large a space, printed itself slowly but at last came out with surprising clearness.

E. H. TRAIN and coloring assistant in his Helena, Montana, gallery.

Galleries West

PACIFIC COAST
1850-1875

ERENS GIGANTIUS, cactus of Arizona desert. Watkins photo.

THE LURE OF GOLD–1849 • San Francisco

CARLETON E. WATKINS

"Views of Yosemite, the Mammoth Groves, Geysers, the Pacific Railroad and Columbia River," read Watkins' advertisement in the San Francisco Directory of 1873. "To obtain them Mr. Watkins has spent several of the best years of his life camping beside mountain streams or laboriously toiling to the summit of lofty peaks from which he has beheld, and transfixed on his faithful negatives, some of the most awe-inspiring scenery that the eye of man has yet gazed upon."

Elaborate the phrasing might be but the quality and greatness of Carleton E. Watkins' work has never been questioned, nor has his energy and enterprise, his pioneer sense of destiny in the West and his courage through a long and productive life. In 1867, landscape photographer C. R. Savage said of his photographs: "Among the most advanced in the photographic art, none stands higher than that of Mr. C. E. Watkins, who has produced with his camera, results second to none in either the eastern or western hemispheres."

Long before the Civil War which brought Matthew Brady and his corps of photographers into early prominence, Watkins was making pictures in the Sierras, the redwoods and placer mining camps. In 1861 while the war was raging, he was making a 12-mule team expedition to Yosemite Valley. One of the photographs made on this trip brought a first prize at the Paris International Exposition a few years later. He was a tall figure in his chosen

WATKINS posing as miner washing gravel with rocker, wet plate wagon at right. Very early photo, about 1851.

JAMES MARSHALL at Sutter's Mill where he discovered gold January 19, 1848. Watkins photo.

field, the finest early photographer on the Coast.

His move to San Francisco was as dramatic as that of any miner, adventurer or ruffian who helped mushroom the sleepy village on the sand hills to a fire-breathing boom camp. Watkins was a boy of twenty in Oneonta, New York, born there November 11, 1829, when the gold discovery news was spread over the country. He helped his father run the village inn and developed an acquaintance with another boy, Collis P. Huntington. In 1851 the two made plans to try their luck in the golden gravels of the western California hills. It took months but finally, by wagon trains and walking, they had their first look at the sailing ships on San Francisco Bay.

Watkins found, not gold, but complete fascination with the welter of drifters and grifters, fortune hunters and fortune finders in the raw-edged city. He had no part of the violence and vice but he felt it all around him and thrived on the excitement it created. As a clerk in a Montgomery Street store he came in contact with everyone from fancy ladies to Friends of St. Patrick, including one fine gentleman named R. H. Vance who had a daguerreotype studio in the city, as well as San Jose and Sacramento. A close friend of Watkins in later life, photographer Charles B. Turrill, wrote about the outcome:

"It chanced that the operator in the San Jose gallery suddenly quit his job and Vance asked the young man, Watkins, to go down and take charge of the gallery until he got a new man. Those were the days of the daguerreotype. Watkins went by stage to San Jose, and the gallery was turned over to his care. He knew absolutely nothing in regard to photographic processes, and was simply for the first few days a care-taker of the place. In that town, the great amount of business done in a photograph gallery—or as it was then called, a daguerreotype gallery—was on Sunday.

"On Friday or Saturday Vance visited San

Jose to see how the young man was getting along. He had not gotten a new operator, so he showed the young man how to coat the daguerreotype plate and how to make an exposure for a portrait. This instruction occupied only a few minutes, and naturally did not go into the minutiae of the profession. Vance told Watkins that when the visitors came in on Sunday he could make a bluff at making the exposures and take their money and that when they came back the following week he would have an operator there to make over anything that had to be made over—it being the idea of both that the green young man would not succeed in his daguerreotype operations. As good fortune would have it, he did succeed, however, and no new operator was ever sent from San Francisco to take the place his predecessor had resigned. He remained for a short period operating and entirely conducting the Vance gallery in San Jose."

In 1857 Watkins returned to San Francisco to open his own gallery for portraits and view photography. Almost at once he realized the great opportunity the mountains represented in his work and made a trial expedition into the wilderness of the Sierra Nevadas. Training a capable assistant to take charge of his studio, he made such trips a regular part of his activity. The following year he visited the Mariposa Grove of redwoods and made probably the first photographs of such individual trees as the Grizzly Giant.

During one of the Yosemite trips he inaugurated the use of an 18″ by 22″ camera and with it took photographs of a group of dignitaries which included Schyler Colfax, Speaker of the House, and friends from San Francisco and the East. It was a fortunate occurrence as the views he made brought about, through Congress and President Lincoln, legislation granting the establishment of Yosemite and the Mariposa Grove as California State Parks, and led Watkins to name his San Francisco studio Yosemite Art Gallery. All were made famous.

In 1873 Watkins made a trip to Utah, shipping wagon, horses and photographic equipment by railroad, with the financial blessings of his friend Collis P. Huntington, who had become a railroad executive. The California artist, William Keith, accompanied Watkins and made extensive use of Watkins' views for many oil paintings.

INTERIOR WATKINS' STUDIO ABOUT 1884, the photographer's children, Collis and Julia, appearing in doorway. Watkins photo.

(*Opposite top*) **WATKINS'** wet plate wagon.

TELEGRAPH HILL, San Francisco to the west, 1863. Both Watkins photos.

The photographer visited the Comstock and Virginia City in 1876 and took the scenic views which comprise a large part of the Phoebe Apperson Hearst Collection of Watkins' work. It is thought that on this trip, Watkins met Francis Sneed who later managed his Montgomery Street studio and whom he married on his fifty-first birthday, November 11, 1880. The couple had a daughter, Julia, and son, Collis.

On Watkins first journey to Southern California in that same year, he went to the "end of steel" of the Southern Pacific Railroad and to Tombstone, Arizona. The photographs taken represented some of the earliest views of San Bernardino, San Gabriel, Pasadena, Los Angeles and San Diego. He returned by the old overland stage road by wagon, photographing California missions.

Watkins' last commercial assignment was extensive, making seven hundred views of the Kern County Land Company development work near Bakersfield. This was his first dry plate work, using negatives 8″ by 10″. In the late '90s he began photographing the Hearst Hacienda estate, near Pleasanton for Phoebe Apperson Hearst but ill health forced him to abandon the project.

In poor health and financial difficulties, Watkins was attempting to sell his plates and photograph prints to Stanford University when the 1906 earthquake struck San Francisco. He was partially blind, living with his family in his studio on the top floor of a building on the southeast corner of Ninth and Markets Streets. In the terror of the disaster his wife and daughter were taken to the emergency camp at the Presidio while his son took him to the home of Charles B. Turrill.

It was a violent ending to a bright career. Watkins' entire collection was destroyed in the fire following the quake and he suffered shock at the loss of his life's work. He retired to the ranch near Capay in Yolo County which had been deeded to him through the offices of Collis Huntington. The photographer never regained his normal senses and was committed to the Napa State Hospital at Imola. He lived there until 1916, dying at the age of eighty-seven.

For some fifty years Carleton E. Watkins was California's foremost photographer of the state's natural beauties. On his many trips he usually traveled in a two-horse wagon in which he carried his equipment and developed his negatives. To reach the Mariposa Big Trees and the more remote areas of the Yosemite Valley however it was necessary for him to transport all apparatus and supplies on mule back. Charles Turrill describes his difficulties:

"At that time travel to the Yosemite Valley was difficult and the Valley itself accessible only by very crude trails. At least twelve mules were required to pack the outfit of the indomitable photographer. It must be borne in mind that large glass plates formed a very important part of his equipment. The tent used in coating and developing these plates was a load for one mule. This young man was compelled to take five mules in his train carrying camera, tent, etc., around the Valley with him, from point to point. As each picture was made the tent had to be set up, the plates coated and then immediately exposed and at once developed. Photographic processes were slow, as also the exposure, which must necessarily be prolonged. One of the most beautiful pictures in this early series—a view of Sentinel Rock—was taken in the early morning light, with an hour's exposure, before the sun had risen on that part of the valley. Only by this method was it possible to have stillness among the leaves of the trees. These prolonged exposures will explain why there is no detail in the foam indicated in the waterfalls, as is shown by the rapid processes of today."

Turrill mentions also Watkins' use of the wet collodion process in which the developed negative was printed on albumenized paper, which was the standard method of photography until about 1878.

Collodion was made by dissolving nitrated cotton in a mixture of ether and alcohol, the worker making his own plates at the time he made the picture. He would clean a piece of glass and coat it with collodion in which chemicals were dissolved then place the plate in a bath of nitrate of silver, which formed silver iodide in the collodion film and made it sensitive to light. The plate was exposed in the camera while wet and immediately after removing it, the developer was poured over it. It was then fixed and dried.

"I spent many hours with him (Watkins)," wrote C. R. Savage in an issue of the *Philadelphia Photographer* in 1867, "and found him ever ready to communicate information to the ardent photographer. I was somewhat curious to learn his *modus operandi* for producing his large views in a climate so dry and difficult to work in. After so much attention to photographic ware, porcelain, rubber, and other material, for making baths, I found *his* to consist of pine wood coated heavily with shellac. In addition to this, he uses the water bath, by means of which he can take a greater number of pictures without losing his chances while the light is good. His negatives are taken, developed, and then placed in the water bath until he is ready to finish them. Just think of carrying such huge baths, glasses, etc. on mule back, and you can form some idea of the difficulties in the way of producing such magnificent results."

Watkins' earliest views were made when he was employed by Vance in San Jose and included Mission San Jose and the two quicksilver mines—New Idria and New Almaden. Among the Vance landscape daguerreotypes Watkins found several worth copying by photograph—the views of Mormon Bar on the Merced River and the renowned picture of James Marshall standing in front of Sutter's Mill at Coloma.

Very few of the old Watkins' negatives from 1857 to 1860 have come to light. Prints are found in many private collections but most of the photographic negatives were destroyed in the San Francisco fire. And because glass was hard to come by, Watkins like other photographers of the day probably cleaned off poor negatives or those unpaid for and recoated them for other exposures.

Watkins made hundreds of stereoscopic views and acquired others for sale as this was a very lucrative part of the photographer's business. He bought three hundred made by A. A. Hart of Sacramento, showing construction of the Central Pacific Railroad. He also purchased the official stereoscopes of the Modoc War made by Louis Heller of Fort Jones, California. Most of Watkins' own stereographic negatives were purchased by I. W. Taber, San Francisco photographer, when all of Watkins' property was sold at auction to satisfy a financial obligation.

After this setback, he built his business up again by retaking many of his stereoscopic views which had been in greatest demand, labelling them "Watkins New Series." To accelerate the remaking process he had a special camera built which used a 5½" by 14" plate on which two negatives were imposed. The landscape views made on 18" by 22" negatives were used in a camera constructed in San Francisco.

(*Opposite top*) **SCHOOL AT SAN JOSE MISSION, 1854,** Bottom, **CONTENTION HOISTING WORKS** and ore dump, town of Tombstone, Arizona, beyond. Both Watkins photos.

(*Above*) **TELEGRAPH HILL, SAN FRANCISCO**, looking northeast, and below, **SANTIAGO MILL** on Carson River, Nevada.

(*Opposite*) **FACADE OF SAN XAVIER MISSION, ARIZONA**. All Watkins photos.

(*Opposite top*) **LONE MOUNTAIN, NEVADA**, 1857. Bottom, **SEAL ROCKS, SAN FRANCISCO**.

(*Above*) **VIRGINIA CITY, NEVADA, AND SUGAR LOAF CANYON**. Below, **THE MOTHER LODE, MARIPOSA COUNTY, 1859**. All Watkins photos.

ADVERTISEMENT in San Francisco directory.

CARLETON E. WATKINS, ill and
almost blind, being led from
his burning San Francisco studio by his son Collis and a
friend, on the morning of April
18, 1906, after the earthquake.

58

WILLIAM J. SHEW

The big, bearded man from New York was nothing if not original and astute. Even before he got to San Francisco he knew the tenor of the place, so fresh and rubbery it would respond to anything new—at least would give anything new a try. And who would want pictures of themelves to send home more than a lot of romantics from the farm thinking they would find gold nuggets rolling in the streets? They had money to get to San Francisco. Maybe he could get some of it legitimately before it was all washed out in the creeks.

So in March, 1851, William Shew went West. Not the long and arduous wagon train way but first class on the S.S. *Tennessee,* crossing the Isthmus of Panama. In San Francisco he studied the people of a dozen nationalities so he would be ready as soon as his photographic equipment arrived on the clipper ship coming around Cape Horn, and spent some time looking over the placer operations at Chinese Camp and Mokelumne Hill. When the ship caught her tug at Golden Gate he was ready for it and in a few days the boom town on the sand hills had something new to gawk at—a photograph gallery on wheels.

William Shew was no Johnny-come-lately opportunist. In Watertown, New York, he was a very early student of M. Daguerre's method of making portraits on metal and took lessons in the art from Samuel F. B. Morse who had invented the new-fangled telegraph. He opened studios one after another in various New York towns without getting much more than curious looks. Then he became intrigued with the posibilities of photography on the frontier, specifically in gold-mad but open-eyed and friendly San Francisco.

Shew saw at once his movable gallery had one great advantage over a room next to some board and canvas segar store. It could be moved away from a fire. In fact, when Shew made the observation, it already had been. The wagon was on the corner of Clay and Dupont and while the flames were licking up every stray sliver of a building there, Shew commandeered a team of horses and pulled his gallery to Portsmouth Square.

This arrangement suited the photographer fine but not the municipal authorities. It was a business in a public park and it would not do to let Mr. Shew think he could claim the property he was sitting on by right of possession. Bowing to a scamper writ, man of enterprise Shew pushed into Brenham Place and succumbed to permanency. He took an apartment in a pretentious building

and a chance on the fire hazard. He lost on both for within a month he was burned out and it was too late to get his four wheels back again.

In William Shew's bright lexicon there was no such word as failure. He moved to Montgomery Street and before long photographers Vance and Bradley began to realize competition was real and earnest. General John A. Sutter and pioneer Jacob P. Leese were seen going into the Shew establishment and then General William Tecumseh Sherman who lived out on North Beachward.

For more than fifty-two years, William Shew stood at his camera and took pictures of the great, the near great, helpless babies on bear rugs and society Semanthas whose only hope of salvation was to get all decked out in ruffled taffeta and have a portrait made that would attract some susceptible coon hunter from Missouri who had struck it rich.

The list was legion. The Shew name graced an elegant likeness of lecturer Ralph Waldo Emerson and one of Thomas Starr King who made an eloquent funeral address over the body of Colonel E. D. Baker, killed in the battle of Edwards Ferry. Both Baker and King had sat for photographs in the Shew gallery.

There were portraits of U. S. Senator David C. Broderick who was mortally wounded in a duel near Lake Merced by David S. Terry; of Kate Batement, the miner's darling; of John Nugent, editor of the San Francisco *Herald;* of General Winfield Scott; of belles and beaux, merchants and nabobs ad infinitum.

Younger men, more aggressive, quicker to learn new photographic tricks, studied William Shew's art and science, then pushed into the field to crowd him out of the upper Kearny Street carriage trade. Yet enterprise and energy kept Shew going and while society was drawn away, he continued with a certain elite patronage, his reputation extending into the Latin and Chinese quarters and the Presidio full of Spanish-American war soldiers.

William Shew was a few months short of eighty-three when he clicked his shutter for the last time. He was proud of his work and his determination. He liked people and liked to bring out character in face and posture. He could retouch negatives with skill and delicacy. He could remember his first picture and glory in his last. He remembered the four-wheel scramble in 1851 and died as a memorable institution of early San Francisco.

(*Above*) **A. A. HART** was noted principally for the views he took along the route of the Central Pacific Railroad in the late '60s. All Hart photos.

(*Top center*) **BANK AND CUT** at Sailor's Spur; (top right) **DONNER LAKE**, Peak and Pass from wagon road; (bottom center) **BUILDING BANK** across Canon Creek; (bottom right) **DUTCH FLAT, PLACER COUNTY.**

CALIFORNIA.

CENTRAL PACIFIC RAILROAD

CALIFORNIA.

CALIFORNIA.

From the William Shew Gallery, San Francisco.

62

ISAAC W. TABER

A man who could buy a thousand pigs in the Marquesas Islands to sell to hungry gold miners at a dollar a pound was not destined to remain a fo'c'sle hand very long. And if he could raise fifty tons of hay for the San Francisco market at a hundred and fifty dollars a ton, he was not going to wash gravel for a long chance on gold.

Yet Isaac Taber became neither a trader nor a farmer but one of the early stalwarts of San Francisco photography. Born in New Bedford, Mass. in 1830, he naturally went to sea. At 15 he was a hand on his uncle's ship, spending a year on a whaling expedition in the Pacific Ocean and Bering Sea. After three more years on the deck and rigging, he joined a gold rush party which took the schooner *Friendship* around the Horn, anchoring at the foot of Clay Street in San Francisco late in 1849.

Taber's shrewd business sense tempered his taste for adventure and instead of straining his back at the gold creeks, he left his party and camped on the sandy slopes of Happy Valley which later would be the First Street area south of Market. For a plan was brewing in his head which he and a few friends believed would be nothing but a dead sure success.

In April of the next year they chartered the bark *Hebe*, sailed to Valparaiso, Chili, for a cargo of old flintlock muskets and kegs of coarse powder, exchanging this in the Marquesas for a thousand native hogs which they discharged in San Francisco. The planners were right. They turned a neat profit with pork bringing a dollar a pound.

There were so many men broken by failure to find gold and this could well have been a challenge to the intrepid Taber. He was flush with some success, why not have a go at the placer beds? Wasn't that what he came out here to do? So the next two years saw him working the gravels of the southern mines near Chinese Camp and then those of the northern area—Mississippi Bar, American

River and Beal's Bar. Finally he went to the region reputed to be rich with gold, Secret Ravine near Rockland.

By 1852 he had mucked in his last stream and bought a ranch in the foothills, which later became part of the Parker Whitney property. The first season he cut fifty tons of hay and sold the crop for $7,500. But farming, he said, was for somebody with less imagination, and he returned to New Bedford a man of experience and wealth at 24.

Photography interested him and he studied it seriously. The deeper he delved the more fascinating the work became and the greater his skill. Settled in Syracuse, New York, he opened a gallery and operated it for a number of years.

When the San Francisco firm of Bradley and Rulofson heard of his work, they invited him to join them. It was an attractive appeal for Isaac Taber to refuse as he had never lost his fondness for the ever new, ever changing city on the Golden Gate. He returned to it in 1864 and worked with the Bradley and Rulofson firm for seven years, then opening a gallery of his own. In that year, 1871, he also married Anne Slocum of Boston. There were two daughters, Daisy and Louise E. who became a writer of special talent with the novels *The Flame* and *Amata*.

The earthquake of 1906 ended Taber's long and successful career. Noted as a portrayer of famous pioneers, noted visitors, of homes and business blocks, he also made many Pacific Coast scenic views which were acclaimed abroad as well as locally. In 1897 he went to London to photograph the grand pageant of the Queen Victoria Jubilee and was later called to Marlborough House to photograph King Edward VII. Isaac W. Taber was 76 when the San Francisco disaster destroyed all his glass plates—twenty tons of view negatives and eighty of his portrait work.

ADVERTISEMENT in Taber album.

64

ACTRESS LILY LANGTRY at Glacier Point, Yosemite. Taber photo.

(*Top left*) **BUILDING AT SACRA-MENTO AND MONTGOMERY STREETS, SAN FRANCISCO.** C. E. Watkins had his studio here in 1871. (Top center) **MISSION STREET FROM THIRD LOOKING EAST, SAN FRANCISCO.** (Top right) **PALACE HOTEL, SAN FRANCISCO.**

(*Left*) **PORTRAITS OF SUSAN B. ANTHONY,** noted women's suffrage leader, and her associate, Anna Shaw.

SAN FRANCISCO CHRONICLE
BUILDING. All Taber photos.

EADWEARD J. MUYBRIDGE

A prodigious photographer of Yosemite Valley and a precise technician, yet a man of capricious temperament, Muybridge attained fame and notoriety as much in court as with his camera. He used three variations of his own name yet did his best work under the pseudonym Helios.

Edward James Muggeridge was his name at birth in Surrey, England, in 1830, and Eadward Muggeridge the one he used in the San Francisco book store which he and his brother Thomas conducted. After traveling for eastern book publishers, he came to the Bay city in the late 1850s at the sug-

gestion of the pioneer daguerreotyper Silas Selleck. At the age of 30 he went back to England, being involved in a stage accident on the overland journey and placed in a doctor's care. When he returned to San Francisco in 1867 it was as Eadweard Muybridge, an accomplished photographer associated with Selleck's Gallery. He began taking Yosemite views at once.

It was no easy task. He went to Stockton by river steamboat, by rented wagon to the Calaveras Grove of Big Trees where he made a number of stereoscopic views. Somewhere along the route he

(*Opposite*) **TUTOKANULA VALLEY** of the Yosemite showing El Capitan, 3300 feet high. Muybridge photo.

EADWEARD MUYBRIDGE in a reflective mood after his labors in Yosemite in 1872.

69

took on his full complement of cameras, cases of glass plates, chemicals, dark room tent, tools, camping equipment, food and firearms. Once again he transferred all this to mules and took the mountain trails behind a guide.

After spending several summer months in this untrammeled wilderness he returned to San Francisco and through Selleck's Gallery issued an extravagantly phrased sales brochure under the name Helios. A quantity of his Yosemite prints were sent to the *Philadelphia Photographer,* the editor reviewing them with high praise which established Eadweard Muybridge as an artist of great technical skill. California publications were equally lavish in their comment.

Muybridge made several other series of views including the redwoods, mining and San Francisco. He accepted commissions from firms and individuals, his most notable one being that done for the U.S. Army on military posts and harbors of Alaska —scenes along the route of the Alaska Steamship Co. as far north as Sitka. It was said these views helped ease the criticism of Secretary of State Seward for the purchase of Alaska from Russia.

In 1869 Muybridge moved his studio from Selleck's Gallery to Nahl's at 121 Montgomery Street, then in something over a year had his own showrooms. In 1871 and 1872 he was identified with Houseworth's Gallery and the following year was with Bradley and Rulofson, the largest photograph publishing and supply house on the Pacific Coast. This firm promoted Muybridge's work extensively to everyone's profit, but due to the photographer's apparently captious move from Houseworth's, there was open bitterness between that firm and Bradley and Rulofson.

Eadweard Muybridge was 42 in 1872 when he married Flora Stone, a San Francisco beauty and divorcee half his age. Within a year the ill-starred union led to tragedy. Returning from photographing the Modoc War, Muybridge suspected his wife of infidelity and after the birth of a son he found reason to believe it was not his child but that of a Major Henry Larkins. He assaulted the man fatally and was arrested for murder. At the trial William Rulofson was of great character assistance and with able counsel Muybridge was acquitted. His wife however died the following year.

Another event to have repercussions occurred in 1872. Ex-Governor Leland Stanford, who controlled the Central Pacific Railroad and a large stable of horses, wagered $25,000 with a friend, Frederick MacCrellish, that race horses in action sometimes took all four feet off the ground at the same time. Through the offices of Bradley and Rulofson, Stanford engaged Muybridge to photograph one of his horses in motion. The first prints made were not too satisfactory but Muybridge had found fascination in the effort and was able to secure an exposure he estimated at 2/1000 of a second with "lightning" collodion. Still later he used more and more cameras until he had a battery of twenty-four placed side by side, the horse breaking the string to each as he passed. As the work progressed Muybridge used fine wires laid across the track in front of each camera. A steel-tired buggy drawn by the horse completed an electrical circuit as it came to each camera causing the shutter to drop.

While the resulting photographs were little more than silhouettes and deprecated by William Rulofson as such, they did show the animals took all four feet off the ground and substantiated Stanford's contention. Muybridge had difficulties with him however and brought suit for $50,000 regarding some precedence of ideas in connection with the theory of animal locomotion.

In his latter years Eadweard Muybridge did extensive photographic work for Pacific Mail Steamship Company in Central America and published three series of documentary books on the Far West. He made further studies in motion at Palo Alto and the University of Pennsylvania, lecturing and writing until his death in England in 1904.

"WILLIAM H. SEWARD" sequoia in Mariposa Grove, 85 feet in circumference, 285 feet high. Muybridge photos.

SAN RAFAEL MISSION, MARIN COUNTY, 1876.

CHARLES L. WEED

Known as the first photographer of Yosemite, C. L. Weed came west from Wisconsin and set up a daguerreotype studio in Sacramento. In 1858 he became junior partner of Robert H. Vance Gallery at 3d and J Streets. In that year he made a trip up the Middle Fork of the American River as far as Forest Hill, on which he made a series of pictures of the placer mining operations.

In 1859 he moved to San Francisco and worked out of the Vance Gallery there. His first trip to Yosemite occurred that year when he visited the area in a party led by James M. Hutchings, editor of the *California Magazine* which later published some of his work. After the party returned to San Francisco, the Vance Gallery advertised the photographs he had taken as "Stereoscopic Views of the Principal Places of the State."

Weed purchased the Vance Gallery in 1861 and operated it for two or three years. When James Hutchings bought the upper hotel in Yosemite, the photographer gave up the gallery to make the hotel his headquarters. It is thought that at this time Weed worked with Carleton E. Watkins in the Yosemite area and that he was less interested in establishing fame and name than in following the rough trails and making his beautiful pictures under exacting conditions.

CATHEDRAL ROCKS AND SPIRES IN YOSEMITE, June 1859. Weed photo.

(*Above*) **THE POND IN PLACER-VILLE AREA**—people in Sunday best thought to be for Horace Greeley festivities.

BEARDSLEY AND HITE'S HOTEL IN YOSEMITE, June 22, 1859. Both Weed photos.

74

(*Left*) **TWO VIEWS OF CROM-WELL'S CLAIM**, Maine Bar, Middle Fork of American River—October 1858.

SARDINE CLAIM, Maine Bar, Middle Fork of American River—October 1858. Weed photos.

(Opposite) **BRIDAL VEIL FALLS, YOSEMITE**—June 1859.

(*Above*) **MAIN STREET, PLACER-VILLE**—The Cary House. Horace Greeley and Hank Monk are shown on front seat of first coach—July 31, 1859.

SETTLER'S CABIN near Coloma, El Dorado County, on South Fork of American River in area known as Old Chinatown. All Weed photos.

PUEBLO OF LOS ANGELES

WILLIAM M. GODFREY

When the ship from San Francisco dropped anchor off shore, the half dozen passengers went down the rope ladder to the skiff and were rowed to the beach. The luggage and freight came in on subsequent trips and when it was all collected and loaded in a wagon, the men climbed into a carry-all and started for the Pueblo of Los Angeles.

William Godfrey was one of them and it is not to be expected he was elated at the flat monotony of the vista which had until recently been under Spanish rule. Godfrey had been disappointed in the gold fields of the Sacramento but San Francisco was a bustling, bawdy place where something happened every time a wind or fog came up. This Los Angeles in 1854 was a sleepy, languid place still partially controlled by the Spanish aristocrats, *los gentes de razon*, who were taking a firmer hold all the time. This was a city of adobe houses set in

swirling clouds of dust churned up by countless horsemen and ox-drawn carretas, except in the Pueblo itself which was cut by a network of canals carrying water for the field crops. But William Godfrey liked it well enough to stay.

By 1860 he was proprietor and operator of the Sunbeam Gallery at 55 North Main Street, or Calle Principal, and was the first to photograph the Pueblo extensively. He issued these views as stereographs under the name Godfrey's Photographic Views and included scenes in the beach areas of Santa Monica and San Pedro, his name scratched with a trembling hand on the glass negatives. In the first city directory in 1872, a full page advertisement extolled the virtues of work done by Godfrey and Flanders but there is no mention of the photographer or evidence of his work in later years.

BURLAP TENT where William Godfrey lived and made pictures during camp meetings at Los Nietos, Los Angeles County, in 1869. Chair stands at bedroom door. Godfrey photo.

(*Above*) **DOWNEY BLOCK** on N. Main Street, Los Angeles, 1872. 2nd story sign reads: "Penelon Photographic Parlors," later occupied by both Parker and Payne. Sunbeam Gallery of William Godfrey was in building at right.

PHOTO OF PART OF LOS ANGELES from Fort Hill taken in 1871. Note fountain in plaza of Pico Hotel enclosed by circular fence. Both Godfrey photos.

(Above) **SANTA MONICA CAN-YON IN 1873.**

(*Opposite top*) **DOWNEY'S OLD BLOCK** on Main Street, Los Angeles, in 1870. Lafayette Hotel shows at extreme right. At bottom opposite, hauling sand for the breakwater at San Pedro in 1870.

BUILDING SAN PEDRO BREAK-WATER, 1869. Pile drivers are on flat cars. Timms Point is shown in background right, Dead Man's Island at left. All Godfrey photos.

FRANCIS PARKER

Operating during the same period as Henry Payne, Francis Parker also had his studio in the same building, on the top floor of the Downey Block. He likewise made stereographs—under the name "F. Parker—California Views." One feature of his work however was exclusive. In that day prior to the use of halftone engravings, he supplied photo prints to the newspaper in sufficient number to be tipped on the front pages.

In the '80s Parker moved to San Diego and operated a gallery there under his own name, later Parker and Judd, and still later Parker and Parker.

DOWNEY BLOCK at Junction of Main and Spring Streets at Temple, 1871. Building at upper right is famous Bella Union Hotel. Parker photo.

VALENTIN WOLFENSTEIN

When Valentin Wolfenstein first came to public notice he was employed as a portraitist for Bradley and Rulofson in San Francisco, the largest gallery and supply house on the Pacific Coast. He had brought his talent from his native Sweden and after acquiring experience and a deft artistic touch believed himself capable of operating his own studio. He arrived in Los Angeles in the late '60s and soon showed the small community he had a well developed sense of portrait work and several special skills.

He opened a studio on the second floor of the New Temple Block and obtained the services of Henri Penelon, a French painter and photographer,

for coloring and tinting portraits. In the '70s he purchased William M. Godfrey's Sunbeam Gallery but suffered financial losses in manufacturing and oil producing ventures.

Seeking new surroundings, he went to Guatemala and Mexico where he operated photographic studios and lithographing processes. When his second wife died he returned to Sweden and established a studio in Stockholm. In ill health he embarked on a trip around the world with his son Robert and while in Los Angeles his condition became acutely worse and led to his death. His son arranged burial in the city.

IN FOREGROUND IS TWO-STORY ADOBE TEMPLE BLOCK, replaced in 1872 with three-story brick. This photo of Los Angeles was taken by Wolfenstein in 1869, looking south from North Main Street. Clock tower is on town's first court house, built by Juan Temple.

THE PANORAMA on these facing pages was made by Stephen Rendall May 13, 1869, while still raising goats, the photo project financed by subscription. Later he was a photographic partner of Francis Parker in studio still operating in the 1880s. Rendall is shown as Fig. 14 in top view opposite page.

(*Above*) **HOUSE** marked 1 is site of Hall of Justice Building; 3 is Buena Vista Street; 4 site of County Jail; 62 home of Judge Olivera, later St. Vincent's College. (*Below*) **15 IS DAILY STAR**; 16 Temple Block (south half later City Hall; 17 Market Street; 21 A. J. Henderson's Livery Stable); 24 Court Street; 25 Murat Brewing Co.

(*Above*) **BUILDING** marked 8 First St. Athanasius Episcopal Church—first Protestant church in L.A.; 10 Temple Street; 11 Old Lanfranco Block; 12 Allen Block—later International Bank; 14 photographer Rendall; 22 Bella Union Hotel; 73 Plaza.

(*Below*) **18 INDICATES** New High Street; 23 Masonic Temple; 27 Roeder and Lichtenberger Wagon Shop; 28 A. J. Henderson residence; 29 Mellus residence; 30 George Hansen residence in First Street; 32 First Street; 34 Spring Street; 36 Brick Jail; 37 Council Chamber.

HENRY T. PAYNE

A well-known Los Angeles photographer, Henry Payne operated from the late '60s through the '80s, his studio being in the Downey Block on North Main Street. He specialized in stereographs, issuing them under the name of "H. T. Payne, Semi-Tropical California Views." In 1876 he made panoramic photos of the city to supersede those taken earlier by Stephen Rendall which are shown on the two pages preceding.

Payne's views of the country surrounding Los Angeles were very popular, advertised in the local press as "departures from the City." On these trips he also made appointments for portrait sittings in the cities he visited. Later he expanded his business under the name of Payne, Stanton & Co.

MAIN STREET, LOS ANGELES, from Temple Block. Payne, Stanton and Co. photo.

TWO OF HENRY PAYNE'S views of Los Angeles taken in 1872. At top is northeast corner of Old Plaza with gas works and Plaza Church in foreground.

VIEW OF LOS ANGELES FROM FORT HILL.

FIRST CIVIC PARADE of Los Angeles Fire Department. Payne photo.

San Diego

RUDOLPH SCHILLER

While visiting photographers from San Francisco and Los Angeles may have taken some pictures in the city, Rudolph Schiller was the first to settle in San Diego and operate as a professional.

Born in Posen, Germany, in 1839, he came to the United States and after a short stay in New York, took his family by boat to the Isthmus of Panama, making the overland trip to re-embark on a ship for California. Arriving in San Diego in September, 1868, he engaged in commercial photography in "Old Town," later moving to the area of present day San Diego. After a few years he entered the bookbinding business.

SCHILLER PHOTOGRAPH of Old Town San Diego—1869.

SCHILLER advertisement in San Diego *Union*, May 19, 1869.

OREGON GOLD–1852

Oregon in 1852 was struggling through the initial stages of settlement. Wagon trains were arriving every week, some organized by missionaries, some by friends and neighbors. There was trouble brewing with the hostile Rogue River Indians in the south and west where gold had been discovered the year before. A few trees had been cut for lumber on the Coast and the first Oregon-built steamboat was running from Milwaukie to Astoria, bypassing Portland, an aggressive contender for port business on the lower Willamette River.

In that year the first of Oregon's pioneer photographers arrived from the East, two young men of widely different backgrounds—Peter Britt from Switzerland and the State of Illinois and Joseph Buchtel from Ohio. Both had learned the daguerre-otyping art, both were to become Oregon's foremost photographers of the period.

Several daguerrotypists had preceded them. William H. Jennings made some portraits in Portland and various mining communities and later in Portland were L. H. Wakefield, Smith's Daguerreotype and Picture Gallery, D. H. Hender who made portraits of Dr. John McLaughlin, Governor Joseph Lane, Joseph Meek and Judge Cyrus Olney.

During the activity of Britt and Buchtel in Western Oregon other photographers were operating east of the Cascade Mountains. Franks and Butler had a gallery in The Dalles where P. Holtz and T. M. Wood also made some pictures. In Umatilla City there was the firm of Gibbs and Schofield and in Le Grande, J. R. Ellison.

PETER BRITT photograph of Twin Falls, Snake River, about 1860.

GROUNDS OF HOTEL DEL MONTE, MONTEREY, CALIFORNIA. Britt photo.

Jacksonville

PETER BRITT

After a brief and unsuccessful gold mining exploit on Oregon's Ashland Creek, Peter Britt bought ground in Jacksonville, built a small house with a work room and set about to make a living in the new land as a daguerreotype artist. He was twenty-two in that year 1852 and it was all an exciting adventure. The area was alive with gold miners, supply agents, traders, drifters and prostitutes—a wild and stormy boom camp kept on edge by frequent raids by the Rogue River Indians.

That spring in the company of two young friends he had come West with a camera and British colonizing sense. The son of English separatists who emigrated to Switzerland, Peter expected to be a portrait painter like his father, to study in Munich and take up a slow, tedious apprenticeship. Plans were changed suddenly when Britt senior and a brother decided to go to the United States, and seven years were spent in Illinois.

Several hundred pounds had come with Peter Britt and his friends on the eight-month wagon trip west. Included was a fine German camera purchased from J. H. Fitzgibbon, one of the good daguerreotypists of the country with gallery in St. Louis where Peter had studied. The teacher had insisted the young pioneer take to Oregon the best mechanical means obtainable for his lack of experience in photographic work. Britt later understood how valuable this counsel had been.

He had two aims—to make the finest photographic portraits in the new Northwest and to build a fine "picture" home. He succeeded in both. His work found early recognition and popularity in Oregon and California and he became an outstanding operator, the artistic quality of his scenic photography as good as the best of Savage and Watkins, his portraits beautifully executed. The graceful Victorian house with its spacious grounds gave him equal fame as a horticulturist and landscape architect. After Peter Britt's death the house was maintained by his son Emil and Daughter Mollie, studio

and work rooms serving as a museum which even today attracts many students of photography.

Professional gardeners journey to Jacksonville to stroll through the groves of palms, oleanders and cedars of Lebanon, to peer through the porch glass where oranges ripen in the winter sunshine. They point out that the man with such an artistic flair to his photography was better known for the new plants he introduced to Oregon, for devising methods of culture and that he was the first to grow grapes in the area on any considerable scale and the first to experiment with semi-tropical flowers and shrubs.

In striving to possess the best photographic equipment, the most luxurious and tasteful home furnishings and the most appropriate plantings for his grounds, Peter Britt made frequent trips to San Francisco. He assembled a traveling outfit in a light wagon with canvas top and fitted it with cameras, plates, dark room and camping supplies. This was his conveyance when making pictures of Oregon and California mountains and coast lines as well as of mundane mining claims, business blocks and street scenes in the pioneer settlements.

Taking a camera on field trips was no simple task in Britt's day. Upon one occasion he was asked to photograph a party of men making a trip to Crater Lake, one of Oregon's scenic beauties. It would be the first time the natural wonder had been recorded on plate and Britt was anxious to test out his methods. The party spent three days in a drenching rain and everyone felt thoroughly discouraged although all but one were seasoned to such weather. The exception was an Easterner not used to the rigors of the outdoors under such circumstances. He coughed and sneezed and voiced his discomfort, persuading the others in the party to call off the trip. It was so decided and preparations were started to return when the sun providentially broke through the clouds, the rain stopped and Peter Britt took his pictures.

THREE BRITT PHOTOS of Yosemite
—(*opposite*) Cathedral Park,
(*above*) El Capitan and (*right*)
The South Dome.

(*Opposite top*) **MIRROR LAKE, YOSEMITE,** and bottom, **MARKET AND MONTGOMERY STREETS, SAN FRANCISCO.**

(*Left*) **HOTEL DEL MONTE, MONTEREY** and below, **CLIFF HOUSE, SAN FRANCISCO.** All Britt photos.

PETER BRITT and his first camera came to Oregon in 1854.

(*Opposite top*) PARLOR OF BRITT HOME and bottom, DISPLAY ROOM IN BRITT STUDIO.

(*Below left*) BRITT HOME in Jacksonville, Oregon built in 1860 and below right, FIRST PHOTOGRAPH GALLERY in Oregon, built by Peter Britt in 1854.

Portland

JOSEPH BUCHTEL

It took Joseph Buchtel a year to adjust his personal and professional conscience to life in the busy little river port of Portland, Oregon. Then in 1853, at the age of twenty-three, he became the owner of a photograph gallery and was on his way to recognition as one of the city's best known citizens and dean of its photographers.

Born in Stark County, Ohio, Joseph Buchtel reached manhood eager to see what the West and the Pacific Coast was like and in April, 1852, he joined the wagon train of an emigrant party. Impatient with its delays, he left with a group of men to complete the trip on horseback. He found wages high and jobs plentiful in the interesting new world and for several months worked as a deck hand on the river steamers.

Possessing some daguerreotyping skill and some funds, he purchased the gallery of L. H. Wakefield which had developed considerable patronage. When Buchtel had established the new business soundly he married Josephine Latourette of Butteville and became active in organizing the first Masonic Lodge in Portland. In later years he was sheriff of Multnomah County for two terms, the same length of service as chief of the volunteer fire department.

A notice in an early issue of a Portland newspaper carried this information about Joseph Buchtel's gallery. "He has introduced all new styles of pictures and new patents which have been adapted by other artists including ambrotype photography, patent leather pictures, ferrotypes, sun pearls, pearls on watches, and latterly the mezzotints and rembrandts. He has invented and received patents for the "contact picture" and also for the photograph plate holder. He also holds for this city the patent of the mezzotint. The rooms are at First and Morrison including ladies parlor, reception salon, technical department and a negative room with more than 25,000 negatives of art, biography, history and social life."

(*Opposite*) **TWO ROOMS** in Britt's Jacksonville studio.

(*Top row*) **BUCHTEL** portrait and views.

(*Left*) **JOSEPH BUCHTEL** seated center in group of Masonic officers and opposite, Buchtel at left in carriage as Portland's fire chief.

M. M. HAZELTINE

Attracted to San Francisco during the early Gold Rush days, M. M. Hazeltine found more pay dirt in photography and built up a reputation for portraits and stereoscopic views in his Baker, Oregon, gallery.

His brother, George I. had started overland for Mexico in 1852 but returned to St. Charles, Illinois, where the Hazeltines had lived since leaving the State of New York. Both M. M. and his brother had studied photography and decided on a California venture. They went to New York City for further instruction in camera work, visiting the Crystal Palace Exposition. Taking a steamer to the Isthmus of Panama, the brothers crossed Nicaragua on foot and took a ship to San Francisco, arriving in December, 1853.

For a short time the two Hazeltines operated a daguerreotype shop in San Francisco and made pictures of Yosemite and other mountain areas. The lure of gold proved too strong however and the brothers went into the boom area of placer camps in Northern California, prospecting near Shasta. After some months, with no appreciable results, M. M. Hazeltine left the mining to his brother and moved to Baker in Eastern Oregon and into professional photography.

(*Above*) **TWO HAZELTINE VIEWS** emigrants arriving in Baker City, Oregon and *below*, steam caliope with **Forepaugh Brothers Circus.**

SELF PORTRAIT OF M. M. HAZELTINE, LEFT, AND BROTHER GEORGE I., in cabin on Clear Creek near Shasta in 1857 while working gold claim.

OPENING THE TIMBER—1860 • Seattle

E. A. CLARK

In 1856 E. A. Clark was one of a small group of settlers on the Duwamish River which entered Elliott Bay just south of the clearing in the timber which was Seattle. He had limited use for the camera he brought with him but took one picture which has been preserved, the first ever made of Seattle. He was Justice of the Peace and King County Auditor, dying at Port Madison at the age of 32 in 1860.

Clark was one of a party which attempted to hang an Indian, one of four involved in the murder of James McCormick. Two of the Indians had been hanged, one released and the fourth locked in a room in the sheriff's house since there was no jail. While two men decoyed the officer away from his house, Clark headed the mob that seized the Indian and with a rope around his neck, was ready to haul him up when the sheriff became aware of the hanging and stopped it.

FIRST PHOTOGRAPH OF SEATTLE, MADE BY E. A. CLARK IN 1860—includes area between Cherry and James Streets, from First Street to Third at edge of timber. House in center foreground is that of Henry Yesler who operated sawmill, only industry in settlement, which was at left of camera facing pole shown. Yesler house faces general area of present Pioneer Place. Hillory Butler home is directly behind Yesler's on Second Avenue. At extreme right on James Street is the S. D. Libby house, later that of John Collins. Water flume is shown leading down James Street and turning north.

New Advertisements.

LIGHT! MORE LIGHT!!

SUNSHINE KNOCKED INTO THE SHADE!

Pictures taken in Cloudy or Rainy Weather as well as in Sunshine!

THE UNDERSIGNED HAVING JUST COMPLE-ted his large and extensive SKY LIGHT, and having REFITTED and REFURNISHED his extensive and commodious AMBROTYPING ROOMS in Olympia, would respectfully inform all those who desire good, durable and true PICTURES, that an opportunity is now offered them of securing them at a cost within the reach of all.

Ambrotypes, Melainotypes, and all kinds of pictures pertaining to the art, taken at the shortest notice.

Children taken in ONE SECOND.

Views taken.

Secure the substance ere the shadow fades, Let Nature copy that which Nature made.

Call and examine specimens.

Rooms in Wright's new building, on Fourth Street, one door from the corner of Main.

E. M. SAMMIS.

Olympia, Feb. 8, 1861. 12tf

NOTICE.

AMBROTYPING??

THE LAST CHANCE!!

Secure the substance ere the shadow fades, Let Nature copy that which Nature made.

OWING TO THE GREAT DEMAND FOR AM-brotyping, the undersigned has concluded to re-main at Olympia a short time longer for the purpose of giving all those who desire an opportunity to get their likenesses taken. The community is invited to call soon at the rooms of the undersigned, as he will remain but ten days longer.

All pictures pertaining to the art put up at a great deduction in prices.

Views taken.

Sick and deceased persons taken at their residence. Children and infants taken in one second.

Ambrotypes and Daguereotypes copied equal to the original.

38   E. M. SAMMIS.

SAMMIS ADVERTISEMENTS IN OLYMPIA, W. T. *Pioneer and Democrat,* August 24, 1860 and February 8, 1861.

AFTER OPERATING GALLERY IN OLYMPIA IN 1860 AND 1861, E. M. Sammis established studio in flimsy building at what is now Main and First Avenue South. In 1865 he built the house shown below on the south side of Yesler Way between First Avenue South and Occidental. His gallery was on upper floor, variety store and Kellogg's drug store on street level.

42

This house stood on Yesler, south side opposite the Occide[ntal] Hotel. In the mi[d] 1860s Gardner an[d] David Kellogg had drug store; A.S.T[..]ham the variety store, and E M [Sam]mis the photogr[aphic] gallery. Sammi[s] built the house. He was Seattle's early photographer, tho a man named Clark took pictures here before Sammis.

107

SAMMIS VIEW OF UNIVERSITY OF WASHINGTON IN 1864.

SAMMIS PHOTO OF CHIEF SEALTH, 1865. Washington historian Clarence Bagley recalls the occasion when it was made. "Old Chief Seattle used to hang about the gallery and scrutinize the pictures with evident satisfaction . . . was easily persuaded to sit and it is a wrong impression that the Indians generally were afraid of the photographer's art, considering it black magic. . . ."

Stereographs

Cartes de Visite

TWO STEREOSCOPIC VIEWS—actual size. (*Above*) Summit of Sierras by C. E. Watkins.

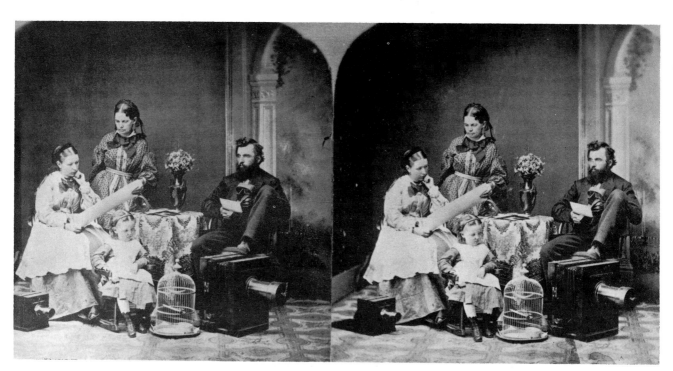

GROUP PORTRAIT BY E. H. TRAIN, HELENA, MONTANA.

"It Seemed Like Everybody Had One"

By nine o'clock frustration had reached the point of no return. And that was Georgie's precise intention—never to return. Here he had come to call on the new girl in town and the evening was dragging like a Bagley scraper. She was black-haired and pretty and her name was Etta and she seemed to want to make friends but how was anybody going to make anything but fidgets when her mother kept pushing that plagued galooken-peeper or whatever it was at him and rattling on—". . . and here, Mister Barnes is this picture of the Rocky Mountain goat. 'Way up there—see? Oh, we like it so much."

But Georgie didn't like it so much at all, not any of the double picture cards in that whole confounded basket. He would never like goats, Rocky Mountains or that funny thing that held the cards while you took it by the handle and put the end with the blinders like on a horse up to your eyes. What did you see but one picture instead of the two on the card? None of this had anything to do with a pretty, black-haired guinea hen named Etta who had just moved into town from Keokuk, Iowa, and was not any more interested in Rocky Mountain goats or Broadway Street in New York on a Rainy Day than he was.

"And—oh, this one—Blondin on the Tight Rope Over Niagara Falls. . . ."

Yet in spite of romance denied, the stereoscope was a universal success and occupied a place in progress as vital as its place in countless homes, in a gilded basket on the center table of the parlor. It was more graphic and imaginative than the family album, gave every mother a chance to get away from the cook stove and into the world and every father a feeling of scientific discovery.

TO OLIVER WENDELL HOLMES the stereoscope was "a leaf torn from the book of God's recording angel."

The stereoscope was also a way of life to craftsmen in the new trade of photography, probably the greatest impetus it had until the advent of the roll film when every man became his own picture master. Skilled photographers made thousands of the double-image cards depicting landscape, event and street scene, which were sold in book and stationery shops the world over. Given sterling approval by Oliver Wendell Holmes who wrote of it poetically—"It is a leaf torn from the book of God's recording angel"—the stereoscope was stock in trade to every picture gallery pioneer.

What the stereoscope did was put depth in flat vistas. To each human eye the object seen is flat. It is only when both eyes view it that the object or scene falls into space, background behind the foreground. In similar manner, the stereoscopic instrument when held up to the eyes allowed them to view two identical images as one, with mind-opening depth. This was achieved because each of the two photographic images was taken at a slightly different angle.

The possibilities of this third dimension viewing were discovered by the English physicist Wheatstone in 1838. He built a stereoscopic viewer and demonstrated it to an enthusiastic field of scientists but it was not until sun light photography came into common usage that his invention proved to have practical worth. Even though a stereoscopic camera with double lenses was in use in 1839, the system reached no popularity until after the expensive and limited methods of Daguerre and Talbot had lived through their twenty-year day. It was the albumen process and the ability to make prints on paper and glass, and the collodion process, which gave the stereograph—the print itself as opposed to the viewing instrument or stereoscope—its big chance in the public eye.

The stereoscopic camera was constructed with two lenses two to three inches apart on the same horizontal plane, corresponding to the center to center distance between the human eyes. Each lens, separated from the other by a wall in the camera, caught the object seen by each eye and transferred it to the single negative so it contained two images each about 3½ inches square. When printed the image on the right hand was mounted on the left side of the card and vice versa. This was necessary for while the print allowed for the inversion from left to right in the negative, the two images were laterally inverted.

It would have been theoretically possible to take stereoscopic pictures with a single camera by moving it, for the second exposure, the exact distance as one eye is from the other, while held on the same plane. But scenes have a habit of changing, however imperceptibly, in minutes and for production purposes such a method would have been imprac-

Hazeltine's Gems of the Pacific Coast

VIEWS OF THE PACIFIC RAIL ROAD.

Baker City, Oregon.

STEREOSCOPIC VIEWS, actual size. (*Top*) Garfield Beach, Great Salt Lake, by M. M. Hazeltine.

(*Center*) **HAZELTINE** and campers at North Powder Lake, Oregon, and (opposite) **UNION PACIFIC RAILROAD** view by J. B. Silvis.

tical. Noted also is the point that even under the ideal conditions afforded by the stereoscopic camera, the two prints were not identical, the right hand print showing a slightly wider field of vision to the right, the left hand print the same to the left.

Stereoscope views were first made in the United States in 1850 with the advent of the wet-plate process of making negatives, and by 1859 their use was widespread. In that year earnest champion Holmes proposed "a comprehensive and systematic stereographic library where all men can find the special forms they particularly desire to see as artists, as scholars, or as mechanics, or in any other capacity. Already a workman has been traveling about the country, showing his employer's pattern in this way, and taking orders for them. This is a mere hint of what is coming before long."

In a second article the essayist gave a description of a modified stereoscope for viewing purposes and the style became a standard thereafter. Holmes' idea consisted of a strip of wood or metal about ten inches long, with two cross pieces and a handle below. The crosspiece nearest the eyes held the two lenses, the one farther away holding the card with its twin views. With slight modifications, this is the form in which millions knew the device.

Just how many millions of stereographs were printed is inestimable. Holmes said in 1861 he had examined perhaps a hundred thousand. The largest producers were in London, Paris and New York, the large supply firms sending out representatives to buy negative production from professional and amateur photographers. In the West, W. H. Jackson, C. E. Watkins, A. A. Hart and many others made a great share of their living with stereograph negatives.

CARTES DE VISITE OF CELEBRITIES BY BRADLEY AND RULOFSON, SAN FRANCISCO IN THE 1870s. Figure in lower right is Admiral Dot, the El Dorado Elf, advertised by P. T. Barnum as "a little love of a man." The Admiral weighed 15 pounds when Barnum discovered him in 1869, was usually teamed for exhibition with Col. Goshen, the Arabian Giant, sitting in the Colonel's huge palm.

"This Is My Sister Fern In San Francisco"

The Ferns and Abigails were proud of their marriages and perky bonnets . . . the Aarons and Jonathans wanted something sentimental to leave mama when they went to war . . . the mountains and mines of the New West had glories for everybody to see—and the cartes de visite, or card photographs, were the way to see them, cheaply.

In Buffalo or St. Louis they were as common as crackers. On Chicago's State Street in 1870 a dozen stores of all kinds displayed them in baskets and colored boxes and spread them out on tables like leaves on the lawn. And people bought them with wild abandon. "Yes, I want these ten and oh, is that Old North Church? And here's General Grant and I want this—the Mona Lisa. And these, of Alaska. How much are they? Twenty for a dollar. Oh my . . ."

The people bought and bought with a suddenly awakened hunger for famous faces and faraway places. Sun pictures were new and had a pleasing smoothness and accuracy of details which the hand engravings in the illustrated weeklies could not supply. And with the broadened interest in showing pictures of celebrities and beautiful scenes to visitors came expanded egos. Anyone could now have a hundred calling cards made just as well with one's own picture on the back as that of Washington Irving, to be left on card trays and pasted in family albums.

The fad gave great impetus to photography. Daguerreotypes, ambrotypes and tintypes, important as they were as the first instance of transferring images to metal, were very limited in use and very expensive. They allowed but one picture where cartes de visite could be made in quantities.

As the name suggests card photographs were first used in France, originating with the Duke of Parma who in 1857 asked a photographer to make him a photograph of a size for calling cards. The novelty came to the attention of Desderi, court photographer to Napoleon III, who introduced the carte de visite to Paris. When the manufacturing process was refined to produce the cards at low cost, thousands were made in France and the fashion spread to London and New York. In 1860, S. A. Holmes in the latter city advertised—"Your photo on a visiting card, London style. 25 copies for one dollar"—and they were issued extensively by George Rockwood and C. D. Fredericks.

Made by the wet-plate process, negatives were prepared by the collodion formula. They required exposures of fifteen to thirty seconds in the studios and with more favorable light, three to five seconds. In large galleries cameras with four tubes were used, each with its own lens and producing its own picture. The plate size, about 6½ by 8½ inches, allowed space for the four images on half its surface, the other half moved into place for a second exposure. Negatives were printed on albumen paper which gave the prints a pleasing gloss. The paper, sized with salt and albumen, was sold dry to the trade, the photographer floating the sheets albumen side down in trays containing the silver nitrate solution.

Printing was a slow process, the paper placed in the printing frame against the collodion film of the negative, and exposed to the sun—the process not possible on dull days. The print was then transferred from the frame to a series of washing baths in a dark room dimly lit by light passing through a yellow curtain, then to a toning bath in a solution of gold chloride. As it came from the printing frame the paper possessed a purple color and successive baths gave it colors of dull red, lilac and finally brown. The last step was the fixing of the prints in a bath of sodium hyposulphate.

The popularity of card photographs continued for thirty years. In the West the pioneer photographers sought negatives of placer mines, Mormon activities, railroad development and curiosities of all nature. People in the public eye were welcomed in San Francisco galleries, most of them requiring little persuasion, and their faces on the calling cards found eager buyers. Watkins, Hart, Taber, Bradley and Rulofson and many others had watchful eyes for actresses, bareback riders, poets, pugilists, politicians, fat men and other freaks. Whatever P. T. Barnum paid to have a picture of Admiral Dot popularized by the distribution of many thousand cartes de visite, he was not heard to complain.

CARTE DE VISITE, actual size, with photographer's advertisement on reverse side.

CARTE DE VISITE, showing Robert H. Vance and staff with advertising of the San Francisco studio on back.

CARTES DE VISITE FROM IDAHO IN THE 1870S. Faces (*top left*) by Leslie and Potter, Silver City; (*top right*) by Isaac B. Currie, Boise City; (*center*) by Bomar and Butler; Idaho City; (*bottom left*) by A. C. Bomar, Idaho City; (*bottom right*) by Bomar and Currie, Idaho City.

DISPLAY OF CARTES DE VISITE BY I. W. TABER, San Francisco photographer in the 1860s and 1870s.

Galleries
in the
Rocky Mountains
and
Western Plains

1858-1875

came on him in August, 1851, since which time he has not even been drowsy. He says he enjoys perfect health and lives happily, and knows no reason for this singular and unnatural phenomenon, and experiences no inconvenience from it. Since his enlistment, he was for a time in the hospital at Philadelphia, and was a subject of great interest to the surgeons of the institution, who set a watch on him for some days, but did not catch him napping. He is now having a history of his life published at Philadelphia. We predict that when he goes to sleep he will take a long nap.—*Wheeling Intelligencer.*

SECRETARY STANTON.—The vituperation that has been poured out against Secretary Stanton has been powerless against the unqualified tributes of admiration freely rendered by Abraham Lincoln, Lieutenant General Scott, Lieutenant General Grant, and other men most cognizant of his public service, and best qualified to judge it. All memory of this abuse will pass away; and the very names of those who vented it will rot and perish. Among the many towering reputations made by this war, few, if any, are composed of more enduring elements than the reputation of Edwin M. Stanton. The staunchness, the tireless industry, Spartan integrity, the gigantic grasp of the Secretary of War in the time of the Great Rebellion will be remembered to the last day of the Republic.

Announcements

TO THE VOTERS OF COLORADO.

In response to numerous letters received from various sections of Colorado, I hereby announce myself as an *Independent Candidate* for Representative to Congress, on the following

PLATFORM:

First.—I stand by, and will sustain and advocate, the reconstruction policy of Andrew Johnson, President of the United States.

Second.—I am in favor of, and will advocate an amendment to the Charter of the Pacific Railroad Company, so that said road shall be located through the State of Colorado, making Denver, and other places in said State, points on said road.

Third.—I am in favor of, and will advocate the passage of a bill by Congress, giving to the prospectors, miners, owners and occupants of mining claims, a title in *fee simple*, from the United States, to their several claims, of every name and nature.

Fourth.—I am in favor of, and will advocate the passage of a bill by Congress, for the payment, by the United States, of all losses sustained by citizens of the Territory of Colorado, from depredations committed by hostile Indians.

Fifth.—I am in favor of, and will advocate the passage of a bill by Congress, for the payment, by the United States, of all debts contracted by the Territorial authorities of Colorado Territory, in raising citizen troops for the suppression of Indian hostilities within her borders.

Sixth.—I am in favor of, and shall insist, that the State of Colorado shall be furnished with more ample and complete mail facilities than has been accorded to her citizens for the past two years.

Seventh.—I hereby pledge myself, if elected, to devote my entire energies to promote the growth, progress, and best interests of Colorado and her people.

On the above *Platform*, I go before the *People* of Colorado, and ask them for their suffrage, and refer my *friends* and

GOLD IN THE ROCKIES–1858 • Denver

RUFUS E. CABLE

A letter from Montana City in 1858 read: "Gold is found everywhere you stick your shovel, paying from five to ten cents to the pan." A pioneer in Auraria said: "This will prove a second California, I have no doubt." And Henry Allen, first postmaster in Denver, wrote: "I panned out forty-five cents worth in one pan full of dirt. I think with the right kind of tools a person can make from five to twenty dollars a day."

This was the kind of talk that brought the people running to Colorado in the late '50s, among them Rufus E. Cable who probably took the first photographs along Cherry Creek which divided the rival settlements of Auraria and Denver, still a part of Kansas Territory. Cable arrived late in 1858 and with a few others was promised two lots if he would build a sixteen-foot cabin on them by March 1 of the next year.

The gold talk was wild but the people in the East were hungry for sensational news after the financial panic of 1857. The stories of Pike's Peak gold turned them from hard times to a chance of wealth in the Golden West. Even a cautious man

in Atlanta, Georgia, would shrug his shoulders and head for the Missouri River. "I ain't got two cents worth of hog fat. Nary a sou to my name, partner. A chance at that gold is all I need."

A chance was all anybody had and a poor one at that. Rufus Cable sold one of his lots and by January he had sixteen of them in El Paso at the foot of Pike's Peak. If he found no gold, he said, he would build houses and maybe go to Arizona or Sonora. He was quickly disillusioned about the gold for he wrote his brother the hidden riches on Pike's Peak would be known very soon as humbug.

But it was all a glorious pandemonium. With the first spring grass every Missouri River boat was loaded to its rickety rails and spilling out the gold-mad emigrants into wagons, hand carts, wheel barrows. Few knew how far they were going or just where and even those probably had provisions for half the journey. But there they were headed for "Pike's Peak or Bust!" Let the Kansas City newspaper writer tell about it.

"Here they come by every steamboat hundreds after hundreds from every place—Hoosiers, Suck-

(*Opposite*) **DENVER NEWSPAPER** advertisements of C. F. Alter and W. G. Chamberlain in 1860.

FIRST PHOTOGRAPH made in Pike's Peak region—a Rufus Cable view of Larimer Street, Denver, in 1860.

ers, Corn Crackers, Buckeyes, Red Horses, Arabs and Egyptians—some with ox wagons, some with mules, but the greatest number on foot, with their knap-sacks and old-fashioned rifles and shotguns; some with their long-tailed blues, others in jeans and bob-tailed jockeys; in their roundabouts, slouched hats, caps and sacks. There are a few hand-carts in the crowd . . .

"Enthusiastic, merry, with light hearts and a thin pair of breeches, they calculate to accomplish all their fonder hopes. Many have sold out all their homes, all their valuables, to furnish themselves with an outfit for Pike's Peak mines. Others left their wives and children behind with no protecting arm or support but what Providence may give, and blindly rush headlong into the blind delusion of glittering sands full of golden eggs . . .

"Only think of 100,000 persons scattered over a few miles of territory, digging and tearing up the ground in search of wealth. Eating greasy meat, sleeping on the cold ground, in rain, snow and hail, hot and cold, wet and dry—up early and late —striving like giants to turn upside down the earth for the sake of gain, away from the cheering hearth-stone, joyous laughter and happy home, among wolves and savage beasts, working out their lives for naught, when, with one-half that energy, industry and perseverence, at home on their farms, they would have full pockets, good health, be with their family and friends, enjoying happiness, comfort and peace."

Like most of the frenzied thousands, Rufus E. Cable did not find gold but he did find some definite direction in life. In June, 1860, he opened an ambrotype gallery on the second floor of the Denver *Herald* Building. The only paper photograph he took then, in evidence today, is the one of Larimer Street looking east from Cherry Creek, although he was purported to have on exhibition a "life-like picture of Kit Carson" and "several handsome photographs and pictures of sceneries, streets and structures in Denver City, Colorado City and other sections of the country.

In October of that same year he left Denver with a man who had been assisting him in the business, Oliver Case, and records would indicate the pair preferred the charms of New Mexico's senoritas to those of Colorado's sceneries.

MLLE. CAROLISTA walking a tight rope over Larimer Street, Denver, in 1861. Photographer Wakely had been actor in troupe with this performer.

GEORGE D. WAKELY

"Mr. George Wakely, from Chicago, Ill., is prepared to make ambrotypes or pictures on leather, for mailing, which can be sent to any part of the world for the cost of a letter only. Perfect satisfaction given or the money refunded."

And with this advertisement in a Denver newspaper October 20, 1859, the frontier settlement on Cherry Creek had a photographer with a gallery and Mr. Wakely was to make himself known here in a number of ways for five years.

When he arrived he was an actor, a member of a theatrical family with Col. Charles R. Thorne's company of traveling players. George Wakely and wife were in the cast with Madame Haydee, Mrs. Wakely's daughter by a former marriage, the leading lady. The two Wakely daughters also took occasional parts.

As a photographer he is best known for his 1861 picture of Mlle. Carolista walking a tight rope across Larimer Street and the ones he took in 1864 of the famous Cherry Creek flood. The tight rope performer had been a member of the troupe when it was disbanded and it has been conjectured that George Wakely was enterprising enough to perpetuate such talent by means of his own. It is safe enough to assume he did not arrange for the flood.

In 1862 he built a small brick building opposite the post office and advertised that his establishment would be "such an enchanting retreat that people will flock in to sit all day in miniature life." The Colorado *Republican* and Rocky Mountain *Herald* were even more effusive: "Wakely is securing those shadows o'er which substance falls with neatness and dispatch . . . so airly and light that it's real fun to sit here for a copy of the human osfrontis."

Early that year Wakely sent to New York for equipment to produce the popular cartes de visite, which were business or personal cards, about 2¼ by 4 inches, with rounded corners and appropriate portraits on the reverse side. When the apparatus arrived, Wakely advertised extravagantly and did a thriving business. He also made a practice of photographing visiting actors in current popularity, such

WAKELY VIEW OF EMPIRE CITY, COLORADO, 1864.

as Mike Dougherty and Jack Lagrishe.

Meanwhile another photographer had appeared on the Denver scene, William G. Chamberlain, and whether or not this competition was responsible, Wakely left the field for a few months. In April of the next year he offered his gallery for sale, pleading ill health and promising to teach the art of photography to any purchaser, assuring his pupil a fortune in a few years. None appeared and the studio closed down for the second time. During this period the ex-actor made a photographic tour of the mining camps including Black Hawk and Red Mountain.

On the night of May 19, 1864, came a fortuitous event for Wakely, tragedy and devastation for the struggling community. A deluge of water came sweeping down the dry bed of Cherry Creek, taking lives, homes and business buildings with it, including the offices of the Rocky Mountain *News*. Wakely set up his camera on the morning of the 20th and made six exposures of the havoc. In its story, the Denver *Commonwealth* printed the photos with this praise:

> "The views taken by Wakely, on Friday morning last, are surprisingly faithful in their representations of the wildness of the waters, and the terrible desolation apparent everywhere at that hour. They are six in number."

Yet a week later the newspaper editorialized that "the proprietor of a photographic institution on Larimer Street" who had made considerable money on the sale of six pictures of the flood had not seen fit to subscribe to a fund to construct a footbridge and roadway over the creek. Wakely bristled and sent a letter to Editor Charles M. Farrell containing the heated words: "If you enter my Rooms again, or make any disrespectful allusions to me in your Local Columns, I will whip you publicly on the streets."

The letter was published in the weekly and the editor countered: "The absence of any regular issue of our paper since its reception is the reason we have not paid our respects to the insulting document before this. *We stand on our bottom and do not fear the ruffian threats of any one.*"

Shortly after this photographer Wakely went East in all probability as some of his mountain views were sent from New York to Central City. Then not until 1879 did his name appear in Colorado records, then in the first business directory of the boom camp of Leadville. The next year the photographic firm of George D. Wakely and Ed W. Clements was set up and remained active for a short time.

1864 CHERRY CREEK FLOOD
caused desolation in Denver but
was fortunate turn of events for
photographer Wakely. His six
exposures were used widely in
newspapers with great demand
for prints by public.

TWO WAKELY VIEWS OF EARLY COLORADO—(*opposite*) North Empire in the 1860s and above, Central City in 1864.

(*Above*) **BLACK HAWK, COLORADO.**

BUCKSKIN JOE, COLORADO. Both photos by Wakely.

HENRY FAUL

Black Hawk and Central City were two of the boom camps in the vicinity of the Gregory Lode—the first and most important lode deposit unearthed in Colorado at that time. And very soon each had its photographer to "record events and preserve the scenes for posterity"—Reed and McKenney in Black Hawk and Henry Faul in Central City.

Faul was able, where Rufus Cable failed, to take the miners' mind off gold long enough to have their grizzled features transmitted to plate and paper. Not many of the negatives of that early period have been found, some destroyed by fire and others, as a matter of expediency, cleaned of their original images and reused.

In 1861, he opened a gallery in Central City, jointly owned with Mark Allyn, who, the next month, ran this notice in the Denver *Rocky Mountain News:*

> "BEAUTIFUL PICTURES—Messrs. Mark Allyn and Faul, Daguerrean Artists from Central City and Spring Gulch, are now in our city, taking most excellent ambrotypes and melanotypes of our streets, stores and private buildings. Those here, or in the mountains, who may want to have a true likeness taken of themselves, their stores or dwelling, their mills or their stockyards, to forward to their friends East, had better call on Mr. Allyn, while sojourning here, or Mr. Faul, in Central City, and have them "secure the shadow, ere the substance perish."

Henry Faul had a succession of partners, among them T. G. Saint and John Glendenin, but the touch that reached the people was characteristically Faul's. In November, 1862, he completed a new gallery in Central City where he said he was prepared to furnish fine views of mountain scenery and the now popular cartes de visite and even enlarge photographs to any reasonable size as fine as could be done anywhere. He solicited the portrait trade in the quaint fashion of the times:

> "CONFIDENTIAL—If you want to send your "gurl" your "fotograft," why don't you go and do it? There's Faul in Central and there's Chamberlain in Denver, who are, like the windmill, always ready and prepared to picture on their pasteboard canvas a love of a likeness, which your darling sweetness, be she ever so fastidious, can't find fault with or keep from freezing unto."

A Denver newspaper article of the day mentioned that photography had become one of the best paying professions and that marriage was a big boon to the photographer. "While there is marrying or giving in marriage," it continued, "or adding to the planet's population in any way, the photographer will be patronized. Ye belles that want to discover in days to come how ye looked when you were on it, and you beaux who wish to transmit to your young ones a mirror in which they can take a glance at their daddy as he looked when he was gay and festive, lose no time in be-taking yourselves to Chamberlain or McDonald, in Denver, or to Faul in Central City, and invest in cartes visites."

Faul's "elegant gallery" was thronged on sunny days "with all sexes of the mountain yeomanry and aristocracy," and his albums were filled with "handsome shadows of splendid looking gents and damsels of the mountains. In 1863 he expanded into a new photograph gallery in the Astor House, a building he had just purchased.

Faul did not limit his photography to the yeomanry and aristocracy but made news shots as well. In October, 1863, William S. Van Horn brutally killed one Josiah Copeland and was sentenced to be hung, meanwhile being taken to Denver for safekeeping. In the Denver jail he attempted suicide by breaking the glass from one of the daguerreotypes of his family and using the sharp edge to slash his wrists. The suicide attempt was not successful, the execution carried out as scheduled and Henry Faul recorded the event, probably the first photo made of a hanging in Colorado. The photograph however has never come to light.

Faul, with an unknown assistant was still doing a brisk business in Central City during the first two months of 1864, "securing the shadows of the fair" and unfair. In August he opened "an elegant room" in Denver, near the corner of Blake and Cherry Creek, opposite the Elephant Corral. The last known Colorado reference to him was made in October, at which time he had an assistant named Newbury. It was concerned with a picture of seven Indian chiefs visiting Denver.

THREE HENRY FAUL views of
Colorado in the 1860s. (*Above*)
Black Hawk and opposite top,
Nevadaville.

(*Opposite bottom*) GREGORY CUT
at mouth of Bobtail Gulch,
Gilpin County.

THREE FAUL VIEWS of Central
City, Colorado, in early 1860s.

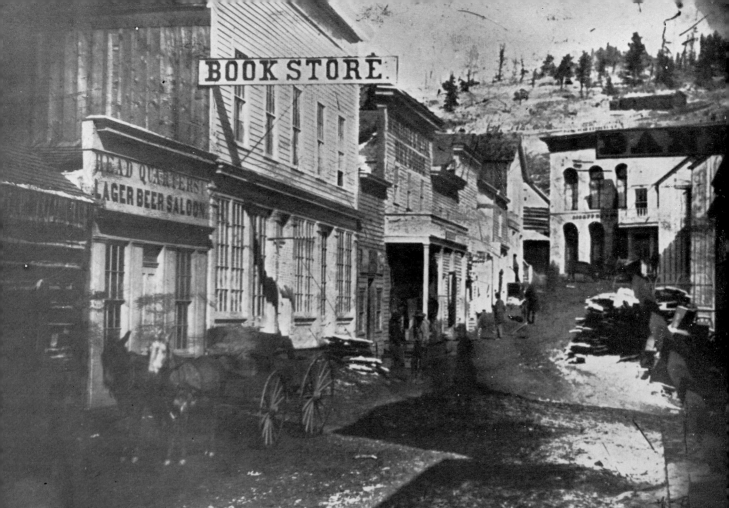

133

MONTGOMERY, COLORADO, in
the 1870s. Faul photo.

WILLIAM G. CHAMBERLAIN

Next to W. H. Jackson, there were more prints of Colorado made by William Chamberlain than any other early photographer. From his first work in Denver during early June, 1861, until he sold his business in 1881, he made great quantities of scenic views and portraits all over the state. His stereoscopic prints, usually marked "Colorado Scenery" or "Rocky Mountain Views" are his best known works although there are many cartes de visite in collections today.

Chamberlain was born in Newburyport, Mass. November 9, 1815, but his family moved to Boston when he was nine. In 1839 he set out to see the world, landed at Lima, Peru, where he became interested in the manufacture of silk and then in mining operations. He remained here until the spring of 1852, during which years he was married and made a visit to the California gold regions. In 1847, he took up the avocation which was to become his life work. He explained his interest in a letter:

"... early in '47 two young men had made a tour through Chili and Peru with a daguerreotype outfit and on their return to the U.S. stopped off in Lima to take daguerreotype pictures; at this early date the sun picture was a marvel and I became interested in the process. Having much leisure from the business on which I was then occupied I was induced to purchase an outfit from them, with some instructions and a little practice for all of which I paid them $300.00. So I became possessor of this art and as a recreation I improved many leisure hours in its practice and became quite proficient in its manipulate. ..."

When Chamberlain moved with his family to Chicago in 1855, he made photography his business, although for a time he was forced to turn to other pursuits since his health was impaired by the use of photographic chemicals. In 1859, he set out for the Pike's Peak gold regions but discouraging reports sent him to California instead. When the

Chamberlain family did reach Denver in 1861, his wife's health demanded that they stay there.

That year Chamberlain made pictures as a "traveling artist" and his first studio was on the corner of what is now 15th and Market. The next year he moved to rooms over Florman's Ice Cream Saloon on Larimer Street, next to the People's Theater, described in newspapers as:

"... an elegant room for taking pictures, a side room which is fitted up as a laboratory, a neat little parlour as retiring room, and a petite lady's sanctum. The suite of rooms is tastefully arranged and fitted up, and in every way qualified for the business for which it is devoted. From the window is a beautiful view of the mountains and the western part of town."

Later that year Chamberlain's patriotism in displaying the American flag moved one of the newspapers to laudatory words. In an editorial headlined "That Flag" the piece read:

"We have a kind of respect for a man who displays the good old flag which has stood

ADVERTISEMENT IN DENVER NEWSPAPER.

the wear and tear of years and which has never been trailed in the dust at the heels of an oppressor, or decorated the triumphal car of a despot; we say we like a man who shows his devotion to his country by displaying the ever glorious flag of our fathers, which they fought so long and so stoutly to plant in that azure field. And for that reason we wo'd ask those of our readers who wish to send their features and forms down to an appreciative posterity by means of Photography, to call at the saloon of Professor Chamberlain, who has thrown the American Flag across Larimer Street, and floated its ample folds to the western breeze. His motto is "A picture or no pay." If the doctors would use a parallel motto, and say "No cure, no pay," we would think some of patronizing them occasionally ourselves."

Chamberlain went on from there, using "A good picture or no pay" in many of his advertisements and his establishment was often described as the place where "the Stars and Stripes" float across Larimer Street.

In January, 1864, he left his Denver studio in charge of Frank M. Danielson who had just arrived from New York City and went to Central City to arrange the opening of a branch studio to be operated by the new man. When he returned to Denver he fitted up a new gallery in the upper story of Graham's new block on Larimer and 15th and took occupancy in November. He remained at this location until he retired from business in 1881.

Through the '60s and '70s he took time from portraits to make annual tours to the mountains, his stereoscopic views selling for from twelve to fifteen dollars a dozen. Mrs. Chamberlain usually worked with the assistants during her husband's absences. When the gallery was enlarged in 1872 the newspaper described it in detail:

"The reception room, with ladies' dressing room adjoining, is situated on the second floor, and is fitted up in a convenient and tasteful manner, exactly adapted to the exhibition of portraits and mountain views. Here may be found pictures of the various grades, from the cheapest to the most expensive kinds, which will enable the patron to make his selection, especially of mountain views, without the trouble or expenditure of time to visit other establishments. The operating room, or glass house, size 24 × 50, is on the third floor and is admirably arranged, having a convenient system of sliding curtains. Backgrounds, of a variety of shades and sizes, adapted to all contingencies, and erected on castors, are here. On this floor are ladies' and gentlemen's dressing rooms. Mr. Chamberlain operates seven cameras, one of which, wrought in exquisite form and valued at $125, and named

CHAMBERLAIN'S gallery on Denver's Larimer Street in early 1860s. Next door was Apollo Theater with balcony. George Wakely's studio was across the street.

CHAMBERLAIN VIEW OF BLACK HAWK, COLORADO, 1867.

the 'multiplying box', has the marvelous capacity of taking, by a simple method of multiplication, seventy-two pictures at one sitting. Mr. Chamberlain has large facilities, an ample stock, and with his long experience, a thorough acquaintance with the details of his business. His success has thus far been commensurate with his reputation as an artist, and he deserves the goodwill and liberal patronage of our people."

William Chamberlain retired from active work late in February, 1881. He sold his portrait and view business to Francis D. Storm but remained at the gallery to give his whole attention to the artotype, a photo-mechanical process particularly adapted to commercial work, such as book illustrations and maps. Storm had been working in the studio as had the son, Walter A. Chamberlain. Soon after the sale, the son worked for W. H. Jackson for a short time, then went to Boulder.

It is difficult for Colorado historians to understand what happened to the thousands of Chamberlain's negatives. Undoubtedly many would have been included with the Storm negatives but these are also non-existent. Chamberlain kept some of the negatives for only a short time, judging by the line on the back of one of his pictures—"Please state if you wish the negative preserved." Part of the negative file was destroyed by fire in the gallery of Charles Weitfle who had paid $200 for an undetermined number of the glass plates.

Legend has one possibility to add. The claim was made many years ago that some old photographic glass plates, said to be Chamberlain's, were in the basement of the Manhattan Restaurant at 1633-35 Larimer Street. The cost to move them seemed so great at the time it was decided to wall them up in one corner. The report, as to whether this was done, has never been verified.

137

CENTRAL CITY, COLORADO, IN THE 1880s.

LARIMER STREET IN DENVER, 1879.
Both views by William G. Chamberlain.

(*Opposite*) **W. G. CHAMBERLAIN'S GALLERIES** in Denver—*top*, on Larimer Street in 1860s and *bottom*, on same street in 1870s.

(*Above*) **PILGRIMAGE** to Mount of Holy Cross, Colorado and below, traveler's camp in South Park, Colorado. All Chamberlain photos.

TO THE PEOPLE
OF THE
CENTENNIAL STATE.

I would respectfully announce that I have added to my already exten-
sive **Photographic Establishment** *numerous different*
accessories *of the best and most expensive assortment, for the*
production *of the very finest* **Portraits**—*having just re-*
turned from the East, where I purchased these necessaries, in order to
compete, in **artistic** *and* **finely finished work***, with the*
very best houses in this or any other country.

I have also engaged the services of **Mr. Terrington** *in the*
capacity of printer and finisher, late of **Mora's famous Art**
Gallery, of New York.

Mr. T. *is one of the very finest workmen in his profession as*
Photographic Printer *and* **Toner,** *and with the able*
assistance of **Mr. A. Rinehart as Operator,** *I am pre-*
pared to **guarantee satisfaction** *to the most* **critical.**

All are cordially invited to call and **judge for themselves,**
as all my work is proof positive of what I say.

The Art Department *is under my personal supervision.*
Enlargements from pictures of any size, in **Ink, Crayon, Pas-**
tel, or Water Colors, *done in the very finest style.*

Very respectfully,

CHAS. BOHM,

284 Fifteenth Street, Denver.

DRY GOODS AND CARPETS.

Foreign and Domestic Dress Goods

Rich and elegant designs, at popular prices, at

DANIELS, FISHER & CO.'S

HOSIERY, GLOVES, NOTIONS AND FANCY GOODS

In qualities suited to the wants of all, at

DANIELS, FISHER & CO.'S

THE BENEFIT OF

Mr. T. M. Tyrrell,

Wednesday Evening, April 8th, 1863.

On which occasion he will appear for the first and only
time in two of his great characters, Bulwer's

EUGENE ARAM

AND

JEREMY DIDDLER,

Sustained by him upwards of five hundred nights in
England and the United States and in which he has
been acknowledged by the press to have no equal.

To strengthen and give greater effect to the drama

Mr. S. M. Irwin & Lieut. L. Gooding

Have, in the most handsome manner volunteered their
valuable services and will appear as

Richard Houseman & Walter Lester.

ap6d2d

STAR OF THE WEST.

To Arms!! To Arms!!!

ALL persons from the age of one month up to one
hundred years, are requested to report to these
headquarters immediately, to

MR. McDONALD

At His New Photographic Gallery,

On Front Street, 4 doors above the Tremont House,
West Denver.

Where he holds himself in readiness to take every
style of pictures of the human face, also views and
scenery of every description.

His facilities for obtaining

THE BEST RESULTS

Are such that he can beat old Photograph himself, or
any other man in this territory.

Particular attention paid to Children. His motto is to
please. Give him a call.

P. S. Particular attention will be paid to taking
pictures of deceased anywhere in the city. Charges
moderate. ap6d1y

BIG FIGHT!!

The great artistic contest between Messrs.

McDonald and Raffle

Will come off on

Wednesday Afternoon,

The 8th day of April, at the HOUR of TWO p. m.
PRECISELY, in the

Pavillion near Parkinson's Ranche.

Seats for the Million,

Will be provided for in good shape at the pavillion
close to town.

Vote for Jas. R. Jones for City Marshal.

—— Mr. Tyrrell's benefit will take place
on Wednesday evening.

—— Go to Miss Kendall's benefit to-
night.

—— Vote to-day for only the men. You
know whom they are. Keep your eye on
the fuglemen, and watch the corners.

—— Vote for John W. Kerr, for Alder
man in the Second Ward.

—— The bath houses of town are doing
a big business during these hot days.

MR. TYRRELL'S BENEFIT.—We direct
attention to the advertisement of the above
named entertainment, and shall take occasion to refer to it more at length to-mor-
row.

RAIN.—There were two or three sprinkles
of rain Saturday evening and for a time the
clouds in the northwest looked very rain-
like. A heavy shower would do a great
deal of good.

—— We understand from S. M. Irwin
that one of our citizens is preparing an address for the occasion of the opening of the
People's Theatre to be spoken by Mrs.
Irwin.

—— When will the mint be started?
when the F street bridge finished? when
this war be over? and who's going to be
elected to-day? are four of the first queries
of interest, whose answers would be read
with much avidity this morning.

PERSONAL—Dr. L. B. McLain and Mr.
Posthoff—the former, Surgeon, and the latter, Sutler, at Fort Garland, have been in

---

143

REED and McKENNEY

For a while it looked as though Albert S. Mc-Kenney would be shaving faces in Black Hawk rather than printing them on photographic paper. In 1866 Black Hawk was a gold camp where the Ute Indians were trying to stop the miners and the preachers trying to stop sin—and Mr. McKenney was trying to get the men to have their pictures taken before either evil set in permanently. When he couldn't appeal to their pride with a camera . . . well, why not with a razor?

The National Gallery of Art was McKenney's grandiose name for his first photograph parlors. Just arrived from the East, he sent out word that his new rooms were "fitted in a most substantial manner, with the best and most improved sky and side lights," his pictures the best ever seen in the mountains and that he was making photographs of men, women and children "by the new instantaneous collodion process."

The Black Hawk public failed to match his enthusiasm and McKenney was forced into business as a "tonsorial artist" for a year and a half. By that time he must have thought his chances with the camera three times as good as before for he opened galleries in both Black Hawk and Central City and a third in Georgetown, promoted by such open-hearted notices as:

> "Get your picture taken before you die or look worse. They are gotten up in the best style of the art at A. S. McKenney's gallery in Central over Hense's jewelry store, and in Black Hawk over Peterson's book store. Give him a call. He can make a tolerably good looking picture from a poor subject."

To augment the sale of cartes de visite and portraits, he floated what was known as a "Gift Enterprise." The tickets sold for fifty cents each and it was said there were no blanks, that some prizes were worth five or six dollars apiece.

Early the next year he was active in his Black Hawk location and in Georgetown—active in more than photography. In December came the announcement of his marriage to Miss Mary F. Bownus of Black Hawk. This may have inspired him to the following appeal:

> "McKENNEY, photographist, has cameras and other appliances that will take a handsome picture of the ugliest man or woman in Christendom, make them look absolutely loveable. That's the kind of an artist to have. Who would be plain and disgusting when they can be made handsome and interesting for a dollar. Pshaw!"

The Central City situation which had bogged down, brightened up when in 1870 McKenney and William H. Reed joined forces in a studio. Reed had been taking pictures there with "the only instantaneous working camera in the country." Now he and McKenney put on exhibition a lot of "Solar Photographs" or portrait enlargements and advertised they had the only "Rembrandt background" in the Territory.

After the sudden death of his infant son and of his wife the next year, during which period the partnership seems to have faded out, the McKenney studio in Central City was struck by a disastrous fire. He opened new quarters in Black Hawk and in 1875 was still making pictures in Georgetown.

FAIRPLAY, COLORADO, IN 1870s.

WINFIELD & HODGES,
(Successors to Frank Winfield)

THE LEADING AND ONLY FIRST CLASS GROCERY HOUSE IN THE CITY OF DENVER.
A VISIT TO OUR ESTABLISHMENT WILL SHOW THE LARGEST, MOST PALATIAL, AND BEST STOCKED GROCERY HOUSE WEST OF NEW YORK.
AND NO WHERE IN THE WEST CAN TOURISTS BE OUT-FITTED SO COMPLETELY. OUR HOUSE IS HEAD-QUARTERS FOR
CAMP SUPPLIES, EUROPEAN DELICACIES AND RARE CONTRIBUTIONS FROM THE WHOLE WORLD.
266 LARIMER STREET, . . DENVER, COLORADO.

(*Above*) **"TRICK PHOTOGRAPHY"**
in Denver business directory.

REED AND MCKENNEY view of
Central City in late 1860s.

Dougan Lost–Who Won?

1868 was a year of Indian uprisings in Colorado but early citizens of Denver no doubt remembered it also as the time San Dougan was lynched and two photographers fought over the privilege of recording the event.

Sanford Dougan was fit for hanging for murders committed in Cheyenne and Central City. A posse in Laramie held him but not tight enough or long enough. Dougan escaped and cheated the noose—for a few days.

Late in November, Judge Orson Brooks, police magistrate in Denver, was held up and robbed by two men. Before the assailants fled, the victim saw them clearly enough to give U.S. Marshal Cook a description of both. It seemed to fit Dougan and an Ed Franklin, well known Denver renegades.

Traced to Golden, where the pair had been drinking and spending freely, the marshal caught Franklin in a half-drunken sleep. He drew his gun but Cook shot first and Franklin's body was brought back to Denver for burial. Dougan eluded the pursuers until he reached Cheyenne where his luck ran out. Taken into custody he was lodged in Denver's Larimer Street jail.

Aroused citizens quickly formed a Vigilante Committee with the avowed purpose of "cooking this fellow's goose once and for all." Marshal Cook learned of the mob's intention and after dark, started the prisoner on a march to a stronger building on the other side of town. The Vigilantes met them on the Larimer Street bridge, overpowered the marshal and seized Dougan.

A cottonwood tree stood handy on Cherry Street between 5th and 6th. A wagon was drawn up under it and standing on it, Sanford S. C. Dougan made his last speech. He admitted the Brooks' robbery and the Central City murder, denied committing the other crimes and begged to be allowed to leave the country. Leave it he did—when the rope went taut and the wagon was pulled away.

Then the Battle of the Cameras began. Photographer Hull heard of the hanging and when he arrived at the scene at daybreak, he found another man setting up his apparatus—presumed to be W. Delavan. Each claimed exclusive rights to the picture but the mystery remains as to which one won the skirmish. Dougan's was the only body removed and both photographers circulated photographs of the man on the rope.

(*Opposite*) **MURDERER DOUGAN** as photographer Delavan saw him, and above is sketch of the hanging and photographers' fracas from D. J. Cook's book— *Hands Up!*

147

W. DELAVAN

"Mr. Delavan, the panoramic artist, wishes us to appeal once more to real estate owners in Denver, to have their property represented in his great "Across The Continent" work. The general view of the town, paid for by the Union Pacific Company, occupying thirty feet of the canvas ($360) and views of churches, public building etc. gratis, occupying eighteen more, and forty-four feet of private views, are all the artist has yet secured. The private ought by right to far outrun the other. The canvas is six feet wide and $12 pays for a lineal foot. Mr. Delavan might quickly fill up his space with views of grog shops and keno rooms, but that neither suits him nor would it us. Denver, at the rate she is going on, is likely to be more slimly represented on the panorama than either Cheyenne, Laramie, Central, Georgetown or Golden City."

This impassioned appeal appeared in several November, 1868, issues of the *Rocky Mountain News* when it seemed a problem for Mr. Delavan to get appropriate views of Denver for his ambitious work. He was attempting to paint a panorama of 6000 square feet, made up of separate scenes in frontier towns from Omaha to San Francisco along the route of the Union Pacific Railroad. The project was to bear the name "Across The Continent" and it was to outshine any promotion of its kind in the West.

It seemed, that added to his painting talents, W. Delavan was a photographer and, the public further learned, a deaf mute. In Central City, the *Register* published this notice:

> "He will take a full and complete view of the town, and says if in obtaining it he is caught falling through somebody's roof or coming out of their cellar, the bill for damages is to be sent to Durant."

However laudable the Delavan effort was, he seems to have found more lasting fame as the man who battled with A. C. Hull over the right to photograph Sanford Dougan hanging from a cottonwood tree on Denver's Cherry Street. Any records showing the completion of "Across the Continent" have not come to light.

DELAVAN PHOTO OF MAIN STREET, TRINIDAD, LOOKING EAST—1867.

148

MORMON COUNTRY–1860 • Salt Lake City

CHARLES R. SAVAGE

It had been thirteen years since the vanguard of the emigrant Mormons looked upon the desert wastelands and foresaw the future glory of Zion. Brigham Young was now threatened with arrest by the United States Government and moved about only with a bodyguard, but the dedicated energy of the saints had worked wonders under the western sun. The irrigated canyon bottoms were now fertile lands. Wages were high, shops busy and Salt Lake City had a population of 14,000.

Into this consecrated activity in 1860 an English convert to Mormonism thrust his own special talents and initiative. He was Charles R. Savage, newly arrived from Florence, Nebraska. He attained no status because of his nationality for almost a third of these colonists consisted of people from Great Britain. What gave the young man an individual cloak was his skill at making pictures of people and things from a box on legs.

Savage was born in Southampton, England, in 1832 and after a disturbed boyhood sought shelter in the spiritual cover of Mormonism, in the Church of Jesus Christ of Latter Day Saints. He moved about Europe in church work and came to New York in February, 1857. Now another interest began to absorb him—making the cheap sun-light pictures coming into vogue on the heels of the expensive daguerreotypes—and he began the study of this art.

Showing a special aptitude he developed camera skills rapidly and two years later moved west to Florence, to begin work as a professional photographer in this frontier area. His first equipment consisted solely of camera, background curtain fashioned from a gray blanket and a large tea chest which served as a makeshift "darkroom."

Florence could not hold a man of his advanced talents and Charles Savage was caught up in the movement west to the deserts and California gold fields and in his own religion and desire to be in the "promised land." He settled in Salt Lake City and found in the Mormon way of life all the outlet he needed for work and inspiration. For forty years he was one of the most widely acclaimed photographers west of the Mississippi River.

Coming out of the Tabernacle on a Sunday, the men in their gray tweeds and women in plain silks and calicos might have seen a man standing by a black box mounted on a tripod. Perhaps the man bowed graciously to a dignified couple with a pretty child, introduced himself and asked them if he might take their picture, explaining that by sunlight he could now put their image on paper. "Well . . . perhaps, Mr. Savage. I know about daguerreotypes but . . . You would like a picture, wouldn't you, Ellen? Are they expensive, sir?"

In the thriving "City of Saints," Charles Savage was first associated with Marsena Cannon, then opened a photograph gallery under the name of Savage and Ottinger, the former the field operator. It was under this name the Savage work gained its greatest prominence. Many of his early negatives were destroyed by fire in 1883 but thousands of the photographs are still in existence.

With a natural feeling for the outdoors, Savage preferred scenic photography to studio work and his views of mountains and rivers appeared on stereographs wherever they were sold. The most widely distributed Savage scene was that taken May 10, 1869, at Promontory Point, Utah, with the completion of the railroad across the continent, a textbook classic. Painted panoramas used in the humorous lecture of Artemus Ward on Mormonism were said to be based on photographs by Charles R. Savage.

In 1866, the photographer made a trip East for new equipment and supplies, going to California and by the water route, returning home across the plains. He detailed the Western trip in a letter to the *Philadelphia Photographer,* writing:

"One of the objects of my visit eastward was to obtain a wagon suited for taking a series of views of the overland route on my return trip. By Mr. Rech, Girard Avenue, Philadelphia, I had a wagon made suitable for the purpose, and shipped by rail and steamboat to Nebraska City. With the exception of being a little too heavy, it answers pretty well. . . . It is about nine feet long and six feet high in the dark room, leaving three feet of space in front for carrying a seat and provisions. The sides are fitted with grooved drawers for the different sized negatives, and proper receptacles for the different cameras, chemicals, etc., forming a very complete outdoor dark room . . .

"With two span of mules and provisions for two months, I joined a Mormon train which left Nebraska City for Salt Lake about the 8th of July. As the Mormon trains are well armed and completely organized, I found it a great advantage, rather than attempt the trip alone, which, by the way, our kind Uncle will now allow anyone to do beyond Fort Kearney.

"We travel more slowly the first few days, and gradually increase our pace until we make about twenty-five miles a day. The modus operandi of managing a train is as follows: About five o'clock the bugle or reveille is sounded to call up the passengers to prepare their breakfast. About six o'clock all hands are called for prayers; that duty over, preparations are then made to roll out; the caravan then travels until about half past eleven or twelve o'clock, then dinner is prepared, then two P.M. the journey is resumed and another camp is made about six o'clock. The night-herders then take charge of the herd, and drive them to a good feeding-ground for the night; supper is then prepared, then prayers by the night camp fires, and orders for the next day's travel are given by the captain, which winds up the day's journey; guards are then placed around the camp, who are expected to keep a sharp lookout for any sneaking red-skins.

"The road from Nebraska City to Fort Kearney presents but few objects of special interest to the photographer. I secured negatives of one or two of the overland stations, and a few rural scenes for any particular features different from the same genre of sub-jects elsewhere. When we reached Fort Kearney it was blowing a gale, but, in spite of that, I made desperate efforts to *take* the Fort, with indifferent success.

"From Fort Kearney on to the crossing of the South Platte, near the present terminus of the U.P.R.R., the road follows the Platte Valley, and a more uninteresting road can hardly be found. Very few trees to be seen, and what with the swarms of green flies and mosquitos, and the strong wind that blows regularly every day, your photographic enthusiasm gets cooled down so much that you see nothing worth taking under the circumstances of such a trip. Added to this, you are never free from Indian attacks, for, at the time of our passing along that route, the few settlers on the mail road were almost scared out of their wits from rumors of Indian troubles.

"Now to photograph successfully on the Plains, you must be perfectly safe from Indians, as on two or three occasions in our efforts to secure some views, we found ourselves alone several miles from the train, and ran one or two risks of being gobbled up by a few stray rascals who are always on the lookout for a weak party, and generally manage to pounce down on a few defenseless wagons that happen to be passing. The sad fate of your former correspondent, Mr. Glovers, shows how uncertain is life in such a place, and the wisdom of keeping a good lookout. The necessary conditions for success under such circumstances are, that you must have plenty of time at your disposal, a strong party well armed with Henry rifles, and good animals."

MONUMENT TO CHARLES R. SAVAGE at southeast corner of Temple Square, Salt Lake City. Inscription on plaque reads: "In affectionate remembrance of Charles R. Savage and in reverential regard for the old folks whose happiness he so greatly promoted through the establishment of Old Folks Day in Utah."

PIONEER FARMS in Emigrant Canyon—Savage photo.

(*Above*) **FOUNDATION OF MOR-MON TEMPLE**, Salt Lake city, about 1867.

(*Above*) **BLACK ROCK** with An-telope Island in distance, in Great Salt Lake.

TEMPLE SQUARE, 1889. Savage Art Bazaar was under canopy on Main Street. Mormon Church buildings, left to right—Assembly Hall, Tabernacle, Temple. All Savage photos.

MAGIC BRIDGE built by Mormon pioneers over Weber River at Peterson, Utah.

(*Above*) **ASSEMBLY HALL, TEMPLE BLOCK.**

(*Right*) **SALT LAKE CITY** from the west, 1880. Tabernacle completed, Temple under construction.

(*Above*) **FORT DOUGLAS**, established in 1864 to protect pioneers from Indians and the "Gentile" whites from the Mormons. All Savage photos.

(*Above*) **GENERAL FREMONT'S HEADQUARTERS,** Santa Barbara, California.

(*Right*) **STAGE STATION IN IDAHO.**

UNIDENTIFIED SCENE under shadow of Wasatch Mountains.

WASHINGTON AVENUE, OGDEN,
UTAH. All Savage photos.

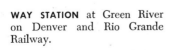

EAGLE GATE entrance to Brigham Young properties.

WAY STATION at Green River on Denver and Rio Grande Railway.

(*Above*) **LOOKING INTO** Utah
Penitentiary from wall. All
Savage photos.

(*Top*) **MAIN STREET, SALT LAKE CITY, 1869.** Photo by Charles W. Carter.

GARFIELD BEACH, GREAT SALT LAKE. Savage photo.

CAPT. A. J. RUSSEL

When peace was restored at the end of the Civil War, Capt. A. J. Russel was one of the Union Army photographers released for civilian usefulness. Not one of the corps on the battlefields between conflicts, he prepared copies of maps and plans in the headquarter posts and took many photographs of Union railway systems and devices.

In 1868 and 1869 he was employed by the Union Pacific Railroad and made many views along the construction route west of Cheyenne as the work advanced, both stereoscopes and whole-plate negatives.

1869 PHOTO OF ENGINE NO. 119 of Union Pacific Railroad on Promontory Point trestle. Note Russel's wet-plate wagon in ravine.

(*Opposite*) **ANDREW RUSSEL** made this photo in 1869 from top of Tabernacle, Temple Square, Salt Lake City, looking east over Tithing Yards. Multi-gabled building is Lion House and beyond, in middle distance, the estates of Brigham Young.

20-MULE FREIGHT TEAM IN SOUTHERN IDAHO.

HANGING ROCK near Echo City, Utah. All Russel photos.

(Above) **LEWISTON, IDAHO, TERRITORY—1863.**

LUNA HOUSE, famous pioneer hostelry, shown in top photo—in 1868.

MAIN STREET IN LEWISTON—1881.

(*Above*) **BLACK JACK MINE AND MILL**, Florida Mountain, Silver City, Idaho Territory.

OLIVER ICE POND, SILVER CITY.
Photo by Hedum and Bishop.

CHARLES R. KINGSLEY

Charles Kingsley was one pioneer photographer who went East instead of West. He was born in Portland, Oregon, in 1857, his father Calvin S. Kingsley, a man of many parts—photographer, the first Methodist minister in Idaho, head of a boys' school and river boat line in Portland. Charles was twenty years old when he came from school in Michigan to Idaho City as photographer with A. C. Bomar.

The two worked together for nineteen years, Kingsley traveling between the small prairie and mountain settlements with an exhibit of his portraits and views. He opened a studio in Boise in 1881 and operated it for several years.

SILVER CITY—court house at left. Kingsley photo.

EXHIBIT OF KINGSLEY PHOTOGRAPHS—was also reduced in size for cartes de visite.

174

(*Above*) **MAIN STREET, BOISE, LOOKING WEST—1881.**

MAIN STREET, BOISE, after 1887 fire—south side of street between 8th and 9th. All Kingsley photos.

TWO PHOTOS BY A. F. THRASHER OF DEER LODGE, MONTANA. (*Above*) First buildings in Leesburg, I. T., 1870.

GEORGE L. SHOUP, standing in front of his home in Salmon, Idaho, with group of Indians. Shoup was last territorial governor and first governor of Idaho as state.

OFFICIAL CAR OF J. B. SILVIS, Union Pacific photographer from 1870 to 1880.

WAGON TRAINS in front of famous War Eagle Hotel, Silver City, Idaho. F. A. Cook photo.

(*Opposite top*) DELAMAR HOTEL near Silver City, Idaho. At *bottom*, WAR EAGLE HOTEL, Silver City, in the 1880s. Photo by F. A. Cook, Winnemucca, Nevada.

179

(*Opposite top*) IDAHO MINES, IDAHO CITY. *At bottom,* MURRAY, IDAHO, IN THE 1880s.

MORGAN GROUP OF MINES, GOLD HILL, IN THE 1890s.

(Above) **THOUSAND SPRINGS**
near Hagerman, Idaho.

TWIN FALLS of the Snake River.

MORE GOLD IN MONTANA–1865

EDGAR H. TRAIN

A man of inventive talents which may have dulled his dedication to photography, E. H. Train was nevertheless one of Montana's pioneer picture takers. He was born in Stockholm, Sweden, in 1831 and as a youth felt the pull toward California gold, crossing the ocean and the American plains to find disillusionment in the glitterless creeks.

In 1864 Train went to Idaho and two years later had a market gardening enterprise in Grizzly Gulch, Montana. But he was now interested in camera work as well as mining, and with A. C. Bundy opened the first photograph gallery in Helena, the first in the state to produce professionally good work. Some of Train's pictures won prizes at the Centennial Exposition in Philadelphia.

Having invented a device for fastening shoes without tying the laces, he spent several years in the East in efforts to interest shoe manufacturers and to market his product. It was without success that he returned to Montana and in 1889 purchased the Utah Assay Office, turning his chemical and geological experience into this phase of mining.

E. H. TRAIN'S HELENA GALLERY
on Cutler Street between Joliet and Water.

E. H. TRAIN working in his Helena gallery.

(*Above*) **TRAIN'S TRAVELING GALLERY** and one of his carte de visite pictures.

(*Above*) **TRAIN PHOTO OF HELENA** looking west from his gallery near corner of Cutler and Water Streets.

DANIEL DUTRO'S homestead cabin and 2-stamp mill on Ten Mile near Helena. Standing by cabin is Little Jack, an old miner. Dutro photo.

DANIEL DUTRO

Continually frustrated in his attempts to lead the active physical life his temperament demanded, Daniel Dutro's health problems finally led him to photography. A Union Army drummer boy in the Civil War against the wishes of his mother, he was sent home to Missouri in a box car to die of pneumonia. He lived to fight with the Vigilantes against such Missouri outlaws as the James boys, Bill Anderson and Quantrell's gang and to help capture one of them.

Dutro was still a boy, seventeen, when he came to Montana in 1867, making the trip up the rivers from St. Louis to Fort Benton. In Helena he was employed as a hod carrier until he collapsed under the heavy loads and worked as a stone cutter, adding a knowledge of mechanics and decorating.

Stricken again, he was advised to stay out of doors and so went prospecting around the Neihart district and the Benton group of silver producing mines.

When his health forced him to a lower altitude, he moved to Fort Benton as a geologist, taking up photography and painting. With partner Roland Reed, he also conducted a gallery in Havre. His uncle, George McBurney built the McBurney House in Deer Lodge and subsequently went blind, Daniel Dutro taking care of him until the patient's death. He then operated a mine at the mouth of Nelson Gulch where he had a small stamp mill and foundry. He discovered Arrowhead mine with rich ore at the grass roots and operated it until his death in 1918, at the age of sixty-eight.

FREIGHT TEAM in front of Daniel Dutro's photograph gallery in Fort Benton. Dutro photo.

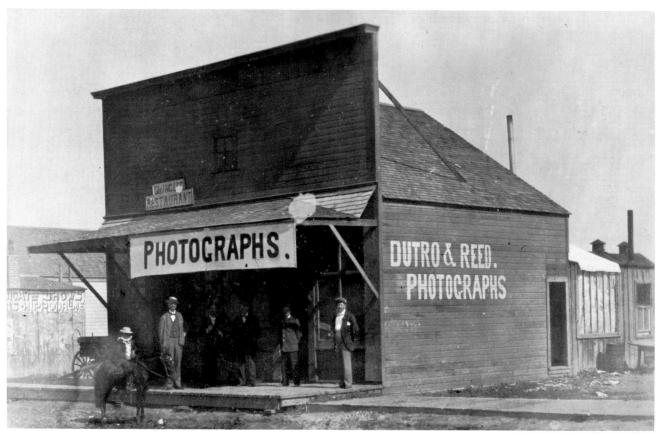

DUTRO'S GALLERY in Havre operated with partner Roland Reed.

PHOTOGRAPHERS OF THE WEST

Incomplete list of photographers operating in the Rocky Mountain area and west from about 1850 to 1910. Those to be included in second volume if possible are given in italics.

CALIFORNIA

LOS ANGELES—William M. Godfrey, Francis Parker, Valentin Wolfenstein, Henry T. Payne, Stephen Randall
PASADENA—*Adam Clark Vroman*
SACRAMENTO—A. A. Hart
Julius Asher, J. R. Hodson, J. A. Todd, S. A. Wolfe
SAN DIEGO—Rudolph Schiller
SAN FRANCISCO—Eadweard J. Muybridge, William Shew, I. W. Taber, C. E. Watkins, C. L. Weed
George D. Morse
SANTA CLARA—*Mrs. Alice Hare*
SANTA CRUZ—*George Webb*

COLORADO

ALAMOSA—*W. L. Williams*
ASPEN—*G. W. Augustine, William R. Augustine*
BOULDER—*Lawrence P. Bass, F. H. Hosier, Joseph B. Sturtevant*
CENTRAL CITY—Henry Faul
Gustave R. Appel, T. G. Saint
COLORADO SPRINGS—*William A. Billman, Alfred Freeman, W. E. Hook, H. L. Stiles*
DENVER—Rufus E. Cable, George D. Wakely, William G. Chamberlain, Reed and McKenney, W. Delavan, Duhem Brothers, William H. Jackson
Charles W. Anderson & Co., Gustave R. Appel, Julian M. Avery, E. W. Baker, George Baldwin, J. E. Beebe, Charles Bohm, Percy E. Brooks, Joseph M. Collier, W. C. Fraser, William J. Gillen, John Green, Charles A. Nast, Frederick E. Post, Alfred E. Rinehart, Henry W. Watson
DURANGO—*J. A. Baston*
GEORGETOWN—*R. F. Elliott, Alexander Martin*
GOLDEN—*M. J. Armentrout*
GRAND JUNCTION—*T. E. Barnhouse*
GREELEY—*F. E. Baker*
LAMAR—*J. C. Avery*
LEADVILLE—*Charles W. Anderson & Co., A. E. Bennett, Peter Carlson, Wellington O. Luke*
PUEBLO—*Edwin R. Clark, Stone and Needles*

SALIDA—*C. W. Erdlen*
TELLURIDE—*H. C. Moore*
TRINIDAD—*O. E. Altman*

IDAHO

BOISE—Charles R. Kingsley
I. B. Curry, Horace C. Myers
IDAHO CITY—*H. C. Tandy, Junk and Co.*
SILVER CITY—*Hedum and Bishop, H. E. Leslie*

MONTANA

CHINOOK—*Charles E. Morris*
DEER LODGE—*A. F. Thrasher*
GLENDIVE—*G. V. Barker*
HELENA—Daniel Dutro, E. H. Train

NEVADA

WINNEMUCCA—*F. A. Cooke*

OREGON

ALBANY—*J. A. Winter, J. G. and Orville Crawford, A. B. Paxton*
ASTORIA—*Blancue and Button*
BAKER CITY—M. M. Hazeltine
CORVALLIS—*Mrs. C. M. Striker, Mrs. H. A. Atwood*
THE DALLES—Franks and Butler
JACKSONVILLE—Peter Britt
LE GRANDE—J. R. Ellison
PORTLAND—Joseph Buchtel
I. G. Davidson, Frank G. Abell
SALEM—D. Kenyon, H. J. Willis, F. A. Smith
UMATILLA CITY—Gibbs and Scofield

UTAH

SALT LAKE CITY—Charles R. Savage, Capt. A. J. Russel

WASHINGTON

COLFAX—*G. W. Bechtel*
SEATTLE—E. M. Sammis, E. A. Clark
George M. Moore
SPOKANE—*G. W. Bechtel, J. D. Maxwell, E. E. Bertrand, F. C. Bailey, Milton I. Loryea*
WALLA WALLA—*Brodeck and Co.*

PHOTO CREDITS

Frontispiece—National Park Service, Yosemite
Page 10—George Eastman House
Page 12—Denver Public Library, Western Collection
Page 13—George Eastman House
Pages 14 through 17—Bancroft Library, University of California
Page 18—Denver Public Library, Western Collection
Page 19—U.S. Geological Survey
Pages 20 through 24—Denver Public Library, Western Collection
Page 25 and top page 28—Smithsonian Institution, B.A.E.
Pages 26, 27, bottom page 28 through 38—Denver Public Library, Western Collection
Page 41—Dale Walden
Page 42—Historical Society of Montana
Page 44—Bancroft Library, University of California
Page 45—Society of California Pioneers
Page 46—Bancroft Library, University of California

Page 47—National Park Service, Yosemite
Pages 48 through 57—Bancroft Library, University of California
Page 58—Society of California Pioneers
Pages 59 and 60—California State Library
Pages 62 through 77—Bancroft Library, University of California
Pages 78 through 88—Robert Weinstein and History Division, Los Angeles County Museum
Page 89—Historical Collection, Title Insurance and Trust Co. San Diego
Page 90—San Diego Historical Society
Pages 91 through 97—Oregon Historical Society
Pages 98 through 100—Bancroft Library, University of California
Pages 101 through 104—Oregon Historical Society
Page 105—Bancroft Library, University of California
Pages 106 through 108—University of Washington Library

INDEX